DISTANCE LEARNING

DISTANCE LEARNING
The Essential Guide

Marcia L. Williams
Kenneth Paprock
Barbara Covington

SAGE Publications
International Educational and Professional Publisher
Thousand Oaks London New Delhi

Copyright © 1999 by Sage Publications, Inc.

All rights reserved. No part of this book may be reproduced or utilized in any form or by any means, electronic or mechanical, including photocopying, recording, or by any information storage and retrieval system, without permission in writing from the publisher.

For information:

SAGE Publications, Inc.
2455 Teller Road
Thousand Oaks, California 91320
E-mail: order@sagepub.com

SAGE Publications Ltd.
6 Bonhill Street
London EC2A 4PU
United Kingdom

SAGE Publications India Pvt. Ltd.
M-32 Market
Greater Kailash I
New Delhi 110048 India

Printed in the United States of America

ISBN 0-7619-1441-2 (cloth: acid-free paper)
ISBN 0-7619-1442-0 (pbk.: acid-free paper)

99 00 01 02 03 04 05   8 7 6 5 4 3 2 1

Acquiring Editor:	Peter Labella
Production Editor:	Wendy Westgate
Editorial Assistant:	Renee Piernot
Sage Copy Editor:	Linda Gray
Typesetter/Designer:	Danielle Dillahunt

Contents

Table of Questions	viii
1. Open and Distance Learning Overview	**1**
Introduction to Open and Distance Learning	2
The Role of Technology	3
Levels of Inactivity	3
The 21st Century	5
Multimodel Environments	7
Research Findings	9
2. Open and Distance Learning Concepts and Components	**13**
Concepts	14
Impact of Open and Distance Learning	14
Trends and Issues	14
Elements of Future Education and Training	15
Strategic Issues and Problems	19

New Opportunities	20
Costs Involved in Open and Distance Learning	22
Components: Competencies and Roles	**24**
Identifying Core Competencies	25
Identifying Critical Roles	26
Open and Distance Learning Competencies	27
Recommendations for Present and Future Roles and Team Membership for Open and Distance Learning Programs and Projects	30
3. The Dynamics of the Distance Learning Environment	**35**
Choosing Appropriate Media	**36**
Interconnection Architectures and Protocols	36
Network Topologies	39
Transmission Media	41
Emerging High-Speed Services and Applications	49
Putting It All Together: Choosing Open and Distance Learning Technologies That Fit the Application	**50**
Applications for Distance Learning	**51**
4. Speeding Up Technology Transfer	**75**
Resisting Change Is a Natural Reaction	**76**
Identifying the Barriers: Role of Perceptions	76
Identifying the Barriers: Reactions to Fear	78
Identifying the Comfort Zone: Reducing or Preventing Barriers to Technology Transfer	79
The Problem With Getting Too Comfortable	79
Overcoming Resistance	**80**
Elements of Success	85
A Few Observations About Change	86
Optimizing Familiar Applications	**87**
Adapting Workspace and Room Setups	87
Some Teleteaching Basics	92

5. Designing Instruction for Learning	**105**
What's the Same?	106
Meaningful Learning	106
Models of Teaching	107
Extent of Participation	107
Modes of Learning	109
What's Different?	111
Prepare Yourself	113
Messaging Style	116
Engaging Distance Learners	127
6. Turning Verbal Information Into Visual Communication	**135**
Working With Space	137
Working With Texts and Fonts	139
Visual Relationships: Working With Color, Line, and Graphics	141
Glossary of Terms	**145**
References	**157**
Index	**161**
About the Authors	**165**

Table of Questions

What is distance learning? What is open learning?	2
How has technological change affected distance teaching and learning through the years?	3
Why are open and distance networks growing in today's and tomorrow's educational settings?	6
What do you mean by multimodel? Can you give an example?	7
What does the research tell us about instructors' experiences in this new environment?	9
What does the research tell us about learners' experiences in this new environment?	10
What else can you tell me about the ARCS Model and how it has been applied to distance education research?	11
Why Choose OSI for Your PC-Based Distance Learning Network?	36

Why choose ISDN for your PC-based distance learning network?	43
If this new environment is going to work for me, I need to be comfortable. How do I speed up the process?	87
How do I get started?	88
How can I make my students comfortable?	91
When it comes to teaching, is there *anything* I can do the way I did before? What things are the same?	106
What is meaningful learning?	106
What do you mean by the extent of participation?	107
How do I use what I know about the nature of participation to create a distance education environment that encourages meaningful learning?	108
What's different in open and distance learning environments?	111
What do you mean by "participative teaching methods and techniques"?	124
How do I prepare students to learn from a distance?	127

✋ THE QUESTION:

How can this book help me?

☞ THE ANSWER:

Distance Learning: The Essential Guide is for individuals who find themselves engaged in open and distance learning activities. It has been designed with an applications focus that will provide you with a "quick start" for immediate work needs. Built on an intuitive set of "How do I" questions, the book will help provide you with the foundation needed to teach from a distance. The format of the book is a multimodel approach, combining reading case studies, tear-out worksheets, and checklists:

- To introduce open and distance learning concepts and methods
- To furnish tools needed to adapt to the changing environment
- To help develop technical skills needed to feel confident, competent, and comfortable teaching from a distance
- To introduce instructional design strategies for reformatting existing courses for open and distance learning environments
- To provide the processes needed to move from a basic level of competency to levels of proficiency and mastery

In addition, *Distance Learning: The Essential Guide* contains templates designed to be copied. This "Quick Start Symbol" will identify those pages. These pages and only these pages may be duplicated. No other part of this publication may be reproduced, stored in a retrieval system, or transmitted in any form or by any means, electronic, mechanical, photocopying, recording, or otherwise, without prior written permission of the authors.

CHAPTER 1

Open and Distance Learning Overview

Chapter 1 presents the history and growth of open and distance education, giving the readers insight into the way evolving technologies have been transitioned into existing distance learning formats. This chapter includes research findings from both the instructor and learner perspective. The purpose of this introductory chapter is to bring all participants to the same level of comfort and understanding. By the end of the chapter, you will begin to see the following:

- Why distance and open education are an important part of today's educational settings

- How technology choices affect open and distance learning

- What the past experiences of teachers and learners can teach us

Introduction to Open and Distance Learning

THE QUESTION:

What is distance learning? What is open learning?

THE ANSWER:

The term *distance learning* and/or *distance education* refers to the teaching-learning arrangement in which the learner and teacher are separated by geography and time. Distance learning can be traced to the mid-1800s with correspondence study in higher education. Not until 1972 did the International Council for Correspondence Education (ICCE) coin the term *distance education* to describe the family of educational practices that had sprung up through the years around correspondence education (Moore, 1990).

Traditionally, the term *open learning* has meant an arrangement in which learners work primarily from self-instruction, completing courses structured around specially prepared, printed teaching materials, supplemented with face-to-face tutorials and examinations (Rowntree, 1990). Open learning, therefore, shares the same roots in correspondence study as distance education.

Although distance education designates various forms of mediated teaching and learning, characterized by the dispersion in time, space, or both of learners and their teachers for the whole or parts of the program, open learning indicates a certain philosophy, underlining open entry and access to learning opportunities. The distinction between distance learning and open learning has been that as it evolved, distance learning incorporated technological advances into the teaching/learning process, whereas open learning did not necessarily do the same.

Open learning has become the catchword or slogan used for the same thing as distance education. The proliferation of "open universities," most of which teach at a distance, has not helped to clarify the issue. The majority of teaching and learning activities in distance education are separated in space and time, and the teaching/learning system is fundamentally based on this premise.

However, the term *open* is often used to refer to institutions, such as the British Open University and the U.S. Community College System, which have open entry policies. Manifestly, this is not a necessary feature of a distance education system. For example, of the 850 distance education programs on the U.N. University/International Centre for Distance Education database in 1996, only 22% had no entry qualifications. We must conclude that the overwhelming majority of distance education programs are definitely not open to all but tend to adopt the same selection criteria as other educational institutions.

The Role of Technology

 THE QUESTION:

How has technological change affected distance teaching and learning through the years?

THE ANSWER:

Through the years, the practice of correspondence study took advantage of current technologies, incorporating into the teaching and learning environment the telecommunication technologies of radio and television broadcasting as well as audio and video recording. Today, distance learning environments have continued to evolve with advancing technology, moving toward virtual classrooms where instruction from a host site is delivered to distance sites using a combination of live, two-way interactive audio, video, or both and synchronous/asynchronous computer-based interactions that take advantage of local area networks (LANs), wide area networks (WANs), the Internet, and the World Wide Web (WWW or the Web).

Levels of Inactivity

Figure 1.1 shows the way distance learning evolved through the years and highlights the development of two-way interactive video delivery

4   DISTANCE LEARNING

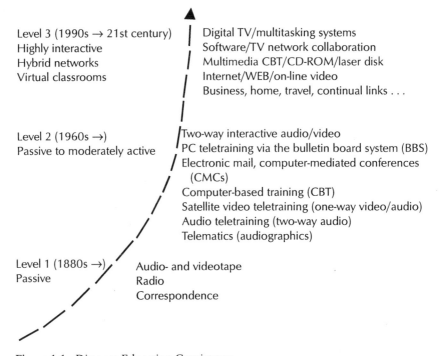

Figure 1.1. Distance Education Continuum

environments. It represents the way distance learning technologies have evolved through the years.

Level 1 consists of printed material, audio- and videotapes, and radio transmissions. Level 1 is considered *passive distance learning* because there is no opportunity for the learner to interact with the instructor in *real time*. We call this type of distance learning environment *asynchronous* because learner and instructor (a) transmit messages "one way" and (b) receive responses after a lengthy delay (mailing, etc.).

Level 2 consists of two-way audio teletraining, one-way video/two-way audio teletraining, computer-based training (CBT) disks, CD-ROMs, laser disks, personal computer (PC) teletraining via the bulletin board system (BBS), electronic mail, computer-mediated conferencing (CMC), audiographics, and two-way interactive audio/video transmissions. Level 2 is considered *passive to moderately active*. We call these distance learning environments *synchronous* because each has the ability to (a) transmit messages simultaneously between sender and receiver (two-way) and to (b) receive immediate feedback and interaction among the distant sites.

Level 3 consists of hybrid environments that combine in one virtual classroom elements of all the distance learning technologies previously described, in addition to the capabilities of the Internet and the WWW. Level 3 is considered *highly interactive.* In these environments, there is no one primary mode of delivery. Instead, the elements of the course being taught determine which technologies will be the "primary" or "instructional" form of delivery and which will be the "secondary" or "support" forms of delivery.

The 21st Century

As we move toward the 21st century, we are seeing more and more hybrid distance learning environments that combine in one virtual classroom the elements of all of the distance learning technologies previously described, including intranets, the Internet, and the WWW. See the following examples:

> Not long ago, point to point and limited multi-point videoconferencing was the way the business of education was done. As we move closer and closer to establishing standards for video over the Internet, Webcasting—simultaneously broadcasting a videoconference locally and over the Internet—is where we are moving. And although PCs were not designed to be a broadcast medium, advances in communication software, high-speed modems, and global transmission networks are providing the framework that will allow the Internet to function more like interactive television in tomorrow's virtual classroom. (Paul, 1998, p. 16)

> Microsoft software and NBC TV announced an alliance to advance digital imaging technologies. Anyone who has a television set can now access not only the news but also a complete menu of digital offerings by purchasing the news/computer channel. This channel becomes your window to access the Internet, Web courses, video games, and computer software programs with little more than a keyboard, a mouse, or a joy stick attached to a black box on your TV. Additional multifunctional capabilities allow the reception of digital signals from digital satellite systems, laser disk players, camcorders, or VCRs—between rooms OR across the world.

6   DISTANCE LEARNING

The above examples are possible because of joint ventures between video cable companies and telephone companies that bring fiber-optic capabilities to the home.

 THE QUESTION:

Why are open and distance networks growing in today's and tomorrow's educational settings?

☞ THE ANSWER:

One reason for this phenomenon is an ever-changing worldview that has prompted higher education, business, industry, government, and health care to reengineer the way training and education are delivered. Another reason is a generation of increasingly reliable, flexible, and affordable telecommunications technologies. A third phenomenon catapulting distance education into the national and international educational mainstream is the current technological and educational climate of "just-in-time/just-enough" training (the ability to deliver instruction on demand, any time, anywhere). Because of these changes, the number of distance education networks continues to grow.

Another reason is that advanced networking capabilities are increasing global access to transmission mediums—satellite, VSAT (very small aperture terminal), fiber optics, integrated-services digital network (ISDN), frame relay, and asynchronous transfer mode (ATM). And as the regulations directing worldwide standards of both telecommunication networks and equipment begin to merge, so do local and global initiatives.

A third and very important reason that open and distance learning networks are growing is directly related to the rapid advances in technology that are producing a generation of increasingly reliable, flexible products, directly related to advances in both the PC industry and the communications industry (see Table 1.1).

Because of these advances in technology, network capabilities, and worldviews, the way the world communicates, shares information,

TABLE 1.1 More Reasons Why Distance Learning Networks Are Growing

From a global perspective, distance learning can support the following:

- Creation of a global education and information infrastructure
- Sharing of human and intellectual resources. Increased availability of qualified teachers, physicians, trainers
- Leveling and opening access to quality education across varying economic levels
- Facilitation of "lifelong learning" among cultures, peoples, ideas

From a technical perspective, the industry climate is changing:

- Increased partnering between network providers and equipment
- Increased partnering between vendors, schools, and corporations
- Increased governmental initiatives to fund technology infrastructures
- Increased requirements for accessing information and resources

---

teaches, and learns has changed. The result of these changes has been an unprecedented need for flexible teaching and training environments and for adaptable instructors who not only can adjust to the new teaching distance learning settings but who can help their learners adapt as well.

The key for teachers/trainers is to pick and choose among the existing and new technologies to create a multimodel approach that "fits" their individual teaching needs and methods.

Multimodel Environments

 THE QUESTION:

What do you mean by multimodel? Can you give an example?

8 DISTANCE LEARNING

☞ THE ANSWER:

A multimodel open or distance learning design blends a variety of techniques and technologies—both old and new—that best fit the teaching/training project or situation.

For example, an instructor decides that the primary instructional delivery medium for her course Advanced Debate Team Strategies for CX (cross-exam) will be two-way interactive video, for these reasons:

- Public presentations are integral parts of the training process.
- The powerful, easy-to-use tracking camera is a good self-evaluation tool to help students critique their visual presence.
- The highly developed, split-second audio and video compression capabilities of today's advanced systems eliminate problems with delays—it's almost as good as being there!

The instructor decides that the school's local area BBS with access to the Internet and WWW is an ideal support system for the two-way interactive video classes. Topics to be debated nationally are announced a year in advance. Through the BBS/Internet/WWW, students can collect information for arguments globally and in real time all year long. Here's an example:

> A recent topic for debate focused on China and human rights issues. In a traditional class, students would go to the library and physically research magazines, books, journals, and newspapers. Many of the resources needed would have to be ordered through other libraries; all of this takes time and costs money. With a BBS, students could save time and money by collecting—in real-time—copies of articles and the like from on-line libraries all over the world—by using the Internet/WWW. In fact, most magazines are now available free, on-line, a month ahead of publication; newspapers from all over the world are also available on-line as they are published. In addition, students in one location could use the BBS/WWW "chat rooms" to talk to other students across the United States and across the world in "real-time," collecting real-life case studies and interviews to further support their positions *for* or *against* their resolution.
>
> For the scenario of the American debate student arguing the topic of the issues surrounding China and human rights, imagine how powerful it would be for the debate student to conduct interviews with *citizens of China*, people from other parts of the world who have recently *traveled to or*

worked in China, or both, documenting their real-life experiences and perceptions.

Because of the choices and resources now available through advanced video and computer telecommunications networks, a whole new dimension has been added to the debate process. Time barriers, distance, and cost barriers have virtually evaporated. Doors have been opened that never before existed. Instead of scheduling a debate for students across a particular country, debates among students throughout the world could just as easily be arranged.

Let's continue our example of how a multimodel design using video/BBS/Internet/WWW could support and enhance a CX debate class and the actual debate:

Impromptu current event topics for speeches and/or arguments are a part of the debate process. A typical issue for debate or argument might be related to rain forests in Australia. The process of preparing for these impromptu speeches and/or arguments has depended on hard copies of articles and so on. Each debater carries huge "tubs" of files from newspapers, journals, books, and the like. With the multimodel design that we've described in place, debaters could use laptops to go on-line to research and access unlimited resources in minutes. They could also do a video link to their classmates at home to "brainstorm" about information and ideas, develop presentation/argumentation strategies, and raise different insights and interpretations that might better prepare the debater.

This is an example of a multimodel design, using familiar methods and media along with new methods and media.

Research Findings

 THE QUESTION:

What does the research tell us about instructors' experiences in this new environment?

10   DISTANCE LEARNING

☞ THE ANSWER:

Researchers have conducted many studies comparing teaching from a distance with teaching face-to-face. Most of these studies are anecdotal in nature (Moore, 1990). However, from these studies, it appears that teachers have found the following to be true:

- Quality of learning is as "as good or better."
- Students are highly motivated (appreciate opportunity/convenience).
- Instructors are better prepared and organized.
- Instructional resources are enhanced.
- Collaborative teaching is encouraged.
- It has *not* resulted in replacing of teachers.

The research seems to say that teachers are finding that teaching from a distance is actually making them more aware of their teaching style, their presentation techniques, and their students' needs. Because of this new awareness, most teachers are getting better reviews and feeling better about their teaching. Teachers are also finding that teaching options that may have once been difficult to arrange are now not only possible but easy to do (collaborating with colleagues, arranging for experts in the field to be a part of the class, accessing data from anywhere in the world).

 THE QUESTION:

What does the research tell us about learners' experiences in this new environment?

☞ THE ANSWER:

Although many studies have been conducted that focus on learners and the learning experience, an extensive literature search of distance education survey models revealed that in early 1998, there are no validated models specific to distance education. Several studies, however, have been conducted using modified versions of Keller's (1983) Attention, Relevance, Confidence, and Satisfaction (ARCS) Model.

The ARCS Model was validated in 1983 with public school students and in 1990 with adult learners. Modified versions of ARCS have been used since 1991 in distance education studies. Wolcott and Burnham (1991) modified the model to determine what adult learners at the University of Utah found motivating about distance instruction. Williams (1994) adapted it to evaluate continuing medical courses delivered via two-way interactive video. As studies exploring concepts necessary for establishing meaningful learning in open and distance education grow in number, so will our understanding of open and distance learning.

 THE QUESTION:

What else can you tell me about the ARCS Model and how it has been applied to distance education research?

THE ANSWER:

The ARCS Model is a systematic design process incorporating four sets of associated strategies proving to be important to distance education environments. The variables (individual questions) are assembled into one of the four groupings that correspond to the ARCS Model: *Attention, Relevance, Confidence,* and *Satisfaction:*

Attention: Learners' curiosity and interest are aroused and sustained through external stimulation (organizational and relevancy markers, change, variety, interaction).
Relevance: Learners perceive a relationship between the learning task and the personal value of learning.
Confidence: Learners believe they can successfully accomplish goals.
Satisfaction: Learners experience satisfaction when they are given feedback information confirming expectations regarding the outcome of learning.

Throughout the studies, it becomes clear that things that really make a difference to distance learners in teleteaching environments are directly tied to the elements of the ARCS components (attention, relevance, confidence, and satisfaction).

Even among studies not directly using the ARCS model, various ARCS components are found. For example, when asked, "What really makes a difference in two-way interactive televised instruction," typical learner responses include the following:

- Instructor is enthusiastic.
- Instructor is prepared, informed, confident.
- Instructor keeps students well prepared and well informed.
- Instructor has taken steps to be "accessible" before and after instructional event.
- Instructor has good presentation and teaching skills.
- Instruction encourages interaction and feedback.
- Instruction is clear, easy to follow.
- Materials and graphics presentation are clear, easy to follow. (Dillon, Hengst, & Zoller, 1991; Egan, Welch, & Sebastian, 1991; Fossum et al., 1991; Rupinski & Stoloff, 1990)

CHAPTER 2

Open and Distance Learning Concepts and Components

Chapter 2 takes a global perspective, looking to see how people around the world view the concepts and components that make up an open and/or distance learning environment. Present trends, strategic issues, problems, and new opportunities are discussed. The discussion then focuses on the research that has been done through the years regarding the skills needed for telepresenters, teleteachers, and teletrainers. This chapter also includes the authors' meta-analyses of this research, with recommendations for open and distance learning roles and competencies.

Concepts

Impact of Open and Distance Learning

Distance learning is one of the most rapidly growing aspects of education and training in the world today. The potential impact of distance learning on all education delivery systems, from the primary to the tertiary level, has been greatly accentuated through new developments in information and communication technologies, which increasingly free learners from the constraints of time and space.

During the last two decades, the world has seen considerable growth in education and training. But the world still suffers from intolerable inequalities both at the international level and within nations. Many countries are struggling with limited access to education and training for children and young people and at the same time have to address basic needs of the older generation. Inferior quality and insufficient relevance is a concern in many countries. At the root of most of these problems is the problem of financing an adequate provision of education and training.

Trends and Issues

Trends affecting education and training in most countries include (a) structural reforms in education and society; diversification of the resource base, privatization, and so on; (b) the move toward a more knowledge-intensive economy; (c) increasing integration; and (d) interdependence of world economy. Rapid developments of telecommunications-based information and communication technologies will provide the prime mechanism for ushering in these changes.

Once the technologies are in place, the implementation of a functional distance learning network involves several administrative and organizational components that include (a) statements of mission, purpose, and objectives; (b) unified program, curricula, teaching, and learning strategies; (c) well-developed interdepartmental infrastructure, communication, and interaction; (d) the presence of administrative proponents; (e) policies regarding students, tutors, and proctors; (f) engaging additional staff and outside experts as needed; (g) materials development; and (h) disbursement, reimbursement, and evaluation.

On a more functional level, there are other issues integrally related to using media in distance education. First, the development and dissemination of distance education materials requires adequate resources (money, skilled personnel, equipment, and materials). There is a world of difference between a teacher preparing handouts and overheads for classroom use, where problems of comprehension can be dealt with on the spot, and the development of mediated-learning materials for people studying in more isolated circumstances, where there is no help immediately available.

Next is the preparation of good quality self-instructional material for distance learners, which is difficult and time-consuming. The materials need to be pedagogically sound—in other words, adapted to the situation of the distance learner. Quality and relevance are issues not only relevant to distance education but also to education in general.

Many people think that the words access and success are interchangeable terms. In the end, technology provides only access. It is up to the teacher, trainer, or faculty member to ensure success—whether the medium is videoconferencing, videocassettes, or distance education via computer.

Elements of Future Education and Training

Although distance education designates various forms of mediated teaching and learning, characterized by the dispersion in time and/or space of learners and their teachers for the whole or parts of the program, open learning indicates a certain philosophy, underlining open entry and access to learning opportunities.

Although there are no direct conceptual links between them, the two concepts are often used to describe similar types of educational provision, sharing a common inspiration of access to learning and flexibility of learning arrangements. Under the label of open and distance learning, this book addresses the whole range of related forms of teaching and learning, within both formal and nonformal education and training. Distance education and conventional education are labels covering a wide range of variations and methods. Very often, methods from both forms are also combined. This means that although there may be a clear distinction in theory, the distinction between distance education and conventional education in practice is far from clear. Therefore, it is not very useful to look at distance education in isolation from other forms.

Open and distance learning, like any other mode or approach, is not a panacea. There are both success stories and failures. Many open and distance learning systems struggle with a range of problems and barriers to effective and successful implementation. Some of the more common obstacles and problems are (a) inadequate technology infrastructure, (b) planning and program deficiencies, (c) lack of human capacity and expertise, (d) inadequate economic resources, (e) lack of recognition of educational equivalence, and (f) neglect of learning conditions and cultural aspects.

Sometimes distance learning is used for school-age children and youths who are unable to attend ordinary schools or to support teaching in schools, at both the primary and secondary levels. However, most school-equivalent courses and programs are targeted toward the adult population. In developing countries, distance education for school equivalency is perhaps the only realistic way of expanding educational opportunities to the adult population. In developed countries, there is still a need for this type of program for those who missed out on the conventional system. Tertiary-level distance learning systems also provide educational opportunities equivalent to conventional university and college education.

Both private and public providers have made important contributions to the development of industry and trade. There are many examples of programs for vocational and professional education. In addition to business studies and technician training, one may mention agricultural training and training for public administration and health services as important sectors. Teacher training is a particularly important area.

This teacher training includes both initial continuing in-service training free from constraints of time and place, leading to the benefits of increased access and flexibility, as well as the combination of work and education. It may also mean enrichment in terms of course content and structure, the place of provision, the mode of provision, the medium or timing of the delivery, the pace at which the learner proceeds, the forms of special support available, and the types of assessments offered. It may mean higher quality in terms of cost-effectiveness, accessibility for students, and pedagogical effectiveness. It will also mean a more learner-centered approach with the possibility of new ways of interaction.

This includes both initial training for formal qualifications, in-service supplementary training for formal upgrading, and continuing in-service training in particular subjects and topics. Many examples, particularly from developing countries, show that teacher training at a distance may reach large groups of teachers and have a profound impact on the development of national education systems.

Nonformal education and community development are other sectors where open and distance learning is used. It is often reported that education programs at a distance reach substantial numbers of women, including programs in societies where women lack equal opportunities of participation in conventional forms of education and training. Open and distance learning also lends itself to the teaching of many of the complex issues of the modern world, in which input from a variety of disciplines is necessary. There is also a wide range of projects involving thousands of school children and youths in cross-cultural electronic communication. Some of these are very good examples of how to promote international understanding across ethnic and cultural borders.

Open and distance learning has the potential of generating new patterns of teaching and learning. Linked as it is with development in information and communication technologies, it offers the promise of developing new ways to address learning needs and creating new patterns of information access and application. Open and distance learning may therefore lead to innovation in mainstream education and even have effects beyond the realm of education itself.

Throughout the world, confidence is growing that open and distance learning will be an important element of future education and training systems and may offer some responses to the world's educational challenges. Despite this, financial constraints and cutbacks are also common in this field. Market mechanisms and customer orientation are highly relevant and may lead to rethinking of organizational and structural aspects. Open and distance learning is approaching a state of acceptance within mainstream education and training that will in the future make it part of the repertoire of most educational institutions. The technological development allows for new patterns of access and delivery in education, often linked to new types of demands and new approaches to learning. One of the trends is the emergence of new forms of distance learning based on more interactive telecommunication technologies, with implications of a pedagogical economic and organizational nature. There is a significant trend toward internationalization. There is limited access for a range of reasons, but the "global classroom" has already been demonstrated in quite a number of projects.

The regional overview shows great differences between all regions of the world, although there are also a number of similarities between some of them. Distance learning has existed for about 100 years in the more developed regions and for about one generation in the developing regions.

In the developing world, distance learning suffers from many of the same constraints and problems as education in general. In addition, lack of infrastructure and professional competence in open and distance learning are important barriers. Nevertheless, these forms of education delivery have come to stay. In the Third World, many countries look at open and distance learning as a major means of expanding education and training and increasing the quality of education. Some countries have established major institutions—open schools and open universities—that seem to become cornerstones for their educational systems.

For example, internationally, there has been an expansion in the number of dedicated distance learning institutions and Open Universities. In Europe most European Union countries have or are establishing a state funded Open University offering a wide range of curriculum topics. Internationally, at least 10 countries have mega universities with more than 100,000 active students studying with them at any one time.

However, if one ignores the central and regional China Television Universities, then outside the United Kingdom this development is still dwarfed in terms of student numbers by the distance education programs of other universities. This is not a new phenomenon. As long ago as the end of the 19th century, university departments of correspondence teaching were established in Chicago and shortly after that in Queensland, Australia.

In developed countries, present trends in the field are linked both to the structural problems of education in modern society and to technological development. The needs of extending learning opportunities over the whole life span and the changing demands concerning knowledge and skills represent a challenge not easily met by conventional structures and institutions of education and training. New information and communication technologies seem to have great potential impact on education. Both existing open and distance learning institutions and conventional institutions are eager to develop effective models of application of new technologies and at the same time meet the needs of learners; they do so with variable success. However, more traditional models still survive, and the field shows great variety regarding both technologies and organization.

Strategic Issues and Problems

The inclusion of national policies for open and distance learning in policy documents on education and training is a prerequisite for effective national planning and use of open and distance learning methods. Statements in national policies should address fundamental questions concerning purpose, target groups, resources and infrastructures, relation to the conventional system, measures for implementation, coordination, funding, quality assessment, and recognition. All stakeholders should be included in consultations, and as far as possible, planning should be intersectional. The question of scale has to be addressed, and private sector involvement needs attention.

A successful national launch of open and distance learning requires visible and strong leadership and high-level government backing. Careful planning, including forward planning after the launch, is essential. To help ensure effective implementation, evaluation procedures need to be built in at the planning stage. Planners should also take into account the training needs of staff newly involved in open and distance learning. New institutions need substantial funding to cover startup. A cost-effective operation is one that makes good use of resources; it is not necessarily low cost. A distance teaching institution needs to have sufficient resources to react quickly to meet new demands. To secure coordination, there needs to be a planned, continuing interface between all the national stakeholders in open and distance learning. In many countries, international and regional bodies may have a role supporting and guiding developments at the national level.

One of the major contributions of open and distance learning in developing countries is to teacher training. It has also contributed to the improvement and expansion of basic schooling for youths and adults. In many developing countries, open and distance learning is a very important means of providing higher education.

Its role in nonformal education is also well-known. It plays an important role in qualifying and upgrading key personnel. Institutions of open and distance learning often serve as resource centers for community-based learning and provide an infrastructure for production and distribution of learning materials.

There are, however, some common stumbling blocks for the effective implementation of open and distance learning in developing countries. The lack of funding and problems of sustained support are perhaps the most important ones, having detrimental effects on quality and achievements. Another common problem is lack of human resources with sufficient competence and motivation. The third major problem is technology infrastructure, which prevents the effective use of appropriate technologies. Finally, the lack of strategic planning and coordination may reduce levels of achievement and cost-effectiveness. Important strategies for future development should include harmonization of goals, policy clarification, coordination at the national level, and regional coordination and collaboration. Capacity building is also important, including increased professionalism in planning and management of open and distance learning systems. Other aspects include networking between national stakeholders, better integration between the education and training systems and the proactive sector, and progressive autonomy and capacity of continuing operation after donations have been exhausted.

New Opportunities

Technology is in itself a driving force that should be used for the benefit of education. The technologies used are not ends in themselves. They are used to extend the opportunities of learning to new groups, to make learning more efficient and flexible, and to enrich the learning processes. A variety of technologies are available at different levels of sophistication that may fit quite well to most kinds of requirements. The potential of advanced technologies is linked to the capacity of storing, retrieving, manipulating, and distributing large amounts of information and of speeding up and facilitating communication. All this is achieved in an increasingly integrated way and at decreasing costs. The challenge will be to use this potential according to clear educational and instructional strategies and to integrate the cultural and conceptual developments resulting from new technologies.

Most of the successes of electronic information technologies so far have been in specialized or higher education. One of the major weaknesses has been in facilitating basic education. Developing countries have benefited the least from potential of educational technology. Interactivity is a key element of most of the new services foreseen. These educational technologies are particularly adapted to education and to the communication need of dispersed users but, on the other hand, need reliable networks. For electronic information technologies to be successfully employed in education on a wide scale, major changes will have to be introduced into education systems. New technologies in education imply new relationships between learners and the available information as learners acquire knowledge and build knowledge structures. The education sector should probably organize itself as a major technology customer and partner in services development, although not necessarily as producer of learning materials. The interaction of open and distance learning systems with traditional educational structures may become part of the strategy in this context. For this to be achieved, the roles of different key actors should be considered and redistributed.

There is no single and simple answer to the question about institutional models and structures for open and distance learning in the future. Without doubt, open and distance learning will be adapted and integrated by "conventional" institutions, probably at all levels and in all sectors. On the other hand, there will certainly also be room for other types of institutions, both private and public. New markets and new technologies will impose changes in these institutions as well, and new types of institutions and services will be established. There will also be a continuous need for dedicated open and distance learning institutions (open universities, open schools, etc.) with a capacity for serving very large target groups. Existing institutions will need to develop new types of partnerships and alliances to meet the needs of society in more effective ways than most of them do today. The wealth of experience and competence in existing open and distance learning institutions must be capitalized on in new alliances and structures. This is a challenge not only to institutional leadership but also to political awareness, policy development, and political leadership.

Costs Involved in Open and Distance Learning

It is often assumed that open and distance learning is cheaper than other forms of education and training. As a general statement, this is far too simple. Usually, the cost structure in open and distance learning is quite different from cost structures in conventional types of education. Clearly, when capital investments substitute high recurrent costs, as is often the case in this field, an important factor is shifted in the economy of scale.

It has been demonstrated in a number of cases that large distance learning programs may produce graduates at considerably lower costs than conventional institutions. This depends, however, on a number of important factors. Although conventional education and training show great variation in costs according to subject area and type of program, open and distance learning also varies very much according to use of learning materials, other media and technologies, and types and organization of student support services. It is also necessary to consider the rate of completion of studies.

Most costs studies compare the costs of single-mode distance learning systems with all of conventional systems, but cost studies of open and distance learning used by conventional or dual or multimodel institutions are scarce. The use of advanced technologies for small target groups makes the provision expensive. Most cost studies are also simple cost-efficiency studies that do not take into account broader qualitative and social aspects and perspectives. One such aspect is that open and distance learning systems are often targeted toward other groups, without easy access to conventional institutions. Other benefits are not easily quantified and calculated. Opportunity costs and productivity effects of upgrading the workforce through in-service training should also be taken into account.

In most cases, funding of open and distance learning institutions is different from that of conventional institutions, and there are many arguments in favor of this. On the other hand, if open and distance learning is to be used increasingly by conventional institutions, funding for programs of this type need some harmonization with funding mechanisms for conventional programs. It is quite usual to assume that students in open and distance learning, who are often working adults, should pay a higher proportion of the costs than conventional students do. However, this assumption should be modified according to missions, target groups, and other local circumstances.

The balance of funding from government, employers, and individual students should be carefully considered, being aware that underfunding may easily have negative qualitative and social effects. As open and distance learning becomes a regular feature in the educational system, care should be taken to remedy any unjustified economic discrimination between groups of students.

The end result has been that technology has become a virtual panacea for educational institutions that have purchased equipment to resolve budgetary crises, improve student access, and share limited human resources. Although educational technologies are no longer on the fringe of education, many institutions are not prepared to deal with the consequences of technology in education. Educational technologists advocate that instructional technologies can be viewed as either processes or products. The problem is that many institutions have adopted technology products but have failed to plan for the process changes.

National reports identify the need to improve teacher use of technology in both K through 12 classes and higher education. The lack of appropriate technology use among educators is important because education must prepare learners to succeed in this technological and information-intensive economy. Billions of education and training dollars have been spent to purchase, install, and maintain technologies ranging from data networks to videoconferencing. When appropriately used, instructional technologies are effective tools to redefine and revitalize the learning experience for a diverse student population, including older students who are likely to work and be enrolled part-time. When misused, these same instructional technologies can disrupt the educational process and dehumanize teaching.

Technology is not only changing classroom instruction, it is also changing the composition of the student population. Now more than ever, diverse groups of students are able to come together via technology and participate in classes together. The possibility and ease of cross-cultural exchanges through technology requires that instructors gain a new level of cultural understanding and communication skills. On the North American continent, technology has the potential to link Americans, Canadians, and Mexicans and to enhance the interaction between geographically close countries. However, one cannot assume that close proximity implies cultural similarity. To maximize the potential of cross-cultural exchanges, training and cooperation in the area of cultural understanding and communication must occur.

Components: Competencies and Roles

Open and distance education has become a strategic means for providing training, education, and new communication channels to businesses, educational institutions, government agencies, and other public and private agencies. Predicted to be one of the seven major growth areas in education (Graham, 1992, p. 1), distance education is critical to our geopolitical status as a means of disseminating and assimilating information on a global basis.

Since 1974, there have been eight studies addressing competencies and roles for distance education and training and development (American Society of Training and Development [ASTD], 1974, 1976, 1978; Civil Service Commission, 1975-76; McLagan & Suhadolnik, 1989; Ontario Society for Training and Development, 1976, 1982; U.S. Army, 1974). These studies give insight into the kinds of training programs needed for preparing presenters, instructors, and trainers to make the transition to distance learning environments. A more recent research study identifying distance learning competencies and roles is described by Thach (1994) in *Perceptions of Distance Education Experts Regarding the Roles, Outputs, and Competencies Needed in the Field of Distance Education.*

The core competencies identified as most critical to educational training and development in these nine studies include the following: adult learning understanding, business understanding, organizational behavior understanding, feedback skills, presentation skills, relationship-building skills, and writing skills. Training modules for distance education built around the competencies identified in these studies are designed in such a way that the participants engage in a variety of activities to gain proficiency in critical teaching competencies. In addition to preparing teachers for the changing classroom instruction, the competencies must prepare individuals for the changing composition of the student population, because diverse groups of students are coming together via technology to participate in cross-cultural exchanges.

Identifying Core Competencies

Identifying the core competencies for all the older and new instructional technologies helps to ensure that they continue to be effective tools in redefining and revitalizing the learning experience for a diverse student population, including older students who are likely to work and be enrolled part-time.

Any core competencies identified today must be useful in the future for open and distance developers, managers, administrators, educators, and technicians. Additional competencies must be added and tailored to the needs, settings, and the technology model or models being employed. Table 2.1 provides a complete list of the competencies reviewed in the nine studies described. The degrees of agreement on each of the competencies are presented in percentages.

Ranking of core competencies are grouped below:

1. Competencies listed 51% to 99% of the time:
    - Program design and development
    - Adult learning understanding
    - Needs analysis and diagnosis
    - Determining suitable training needs, methods
    - Individual proficiency—planning and research

2. Competencies listed 50% of the time:
    - Instructional design techniques
    - Identification of job-related training
    - Group and organizational development
    - Management of training and development
    - Identification of competencies
    - Communications skills base:
        ❖ Interpersonal competencies
        ❖ Group process feedback writing

- Visioning, projecting future trends
- Evaluations
- Computer understanding

Identifying Critical Roles

Just as core competencies identified today must be useful in the future for open and distance education environments, so must critical roles of traditional training and education. Table 2.2 presents the training and development roles most frequently identified by seven of the nine

TABLE 2.1 Core Competencies Identified by Experts in Training and Development (in percentages)

Need analysis and diagnosis	88
Determination of appropriate training	75
Program design and development	100
Development of material resources	63
Management of internal resources	63
Management of external resources	63
Conducting classroom training (instructional techniques)	50
Job/performance-related training	50
Individual development planning and counseling	75
Group and organization development	50
Training research	75
Management of working relationship with managers	13
Management of the training and development function	50
Professional self-development	38
Competencies	50
Communication	50
Evaluation	50
Business understanding	45
Computer understanding	50
Visioning	58
Adult learning understanding	60

TABLE 2.2 Critical Roles Identified by Experts in Training and Development

Role	1974 ASTD	1975 Civil Service	1976 ASTD	1976 Canadian	1978 ASTD	1982 Canadian	1989 ASTD
Task specialist	X	X	X		X		X
Team member				X			
Leader/ instructor	X		X	X	X	X	X
Coordinator	X	X	X	X	X	X	X
Liason/ consultant	X	X	X	X	X	X	
Administrator	X	X	X	X	X		X
Change agent	X		X	X	X	X	X

studies previously cited (two studies, the 1974 U.S. Army Study and the 1995 DD&E study, provided no such rankings).

Open and Distance Learning Competencies

Two research studies completed in 1989 and 1994 looked at competencies for training and development and at competencies for distance learning. The first study in 1989, by McLagan and Suhadolnik (for ASTD), *Models for Human Resource Development Practice (the Research Report)* was carried out by distributing 1,010 questionnaires in the United States and compiling the 473 (47%) returned usable surveys. The second study in 1994 by Carol E. Thach (in the United States) was *Perceptions of Distance Education Experts Regarding the Roles, Outputs, and Competencies Needed in the Field of Distance Education: A Research Model*. This study had two rounds of surveys. In the first round, 102 experts were surveyed with 51 (50%) experts completing and returning the survey tool. In Round 2, the survey tool was sent to 51 experts. In this round, 36 (71%) responded, and their responses were tallied.

A visual comparison of the competencies and roles identified as critical in the two studies (McLagan & Suhadolnik, 1989; Thach, 1994) are presented side by side in Tables 2.3 and 2.4.

TABLE 2.3 Training and Development/Distance Learning Competencies Compared

Competency	Training and Development (McLagan & Suhadelnik, 1989)	Distance Learning (Thach, 1994)
Adult learning understanding	X	X
Business understanding	X	X
Career development theory and technique understanding	X	
Change agent skills		X
Competency identification skill	X	
Computer competence	X	X
Cost-benefit analysis	X	
Coaching skills	X	X
Data reduction skill	X	X
Delegation skill	X	
Electronic systems skills	X	
Evaluation skills		X
Facilities skill	X	
Feedback skills	X	X
General education theory		X
Group process skills	X	X
Industrial understanding	X	
Information search skills	X	
Intellectual versatility	X	
Instructional design skills		X
Knowledge of distance learning		X
Learning style and theory		X
Media attributes knowledge		X
Model building skills	X	X
Needs assessment skills		X
Negotiation skill	X	X
Objectives preparation skill	X	

TABLE 2.3 *Continued*

Competency	Training and Development (McLagan & Suhadelnik, 1989)	Distance Learning (Thach, 1994)
Observing skill	X	
Organization behavior understanding	X	X
Organization development theories and techniques understanding	X	
Organization understanding	X	X
Performance observation skill	X	
Planning skills		X
Policy-making skills		X
Presentation skills	X	
Project management skill	X	X
Questioning skill	X	X
Record management skill	X	
Relationship building skill	X	X
Research skills	X	
Self-knowledge	X	
Software skills		X
Strategic planning		X
Subject matter understanding	X	
Teaching strategies/models		X
Technology access knowledge		X
Training and development, theories, and techniques	X	
Visioning skills	X	
Videoconferencing skills		X
Writing skills	X	X

TABLE 2.4 Training and Development/Distance Learning Roles Compared

Role	Training and Development (McLagan & Suhadolnik, 1989)	Distance Learning (Thach, 1994)
Administrator	X	X
Evaluator	X	X
Editor		X
Instructor/facilitator		X
Instructional designer	X	
Individual career development advisor	X	
Graphics designer		X
HRD materials developer	X	
HRD manager	X	
Librarian		X
Marketer	X	
Needs analyst	X	
Organization change agent	X	
Program designer	X	X
Researcher	X	
Site facilitator		X
Support staff		X
Technology expert		X
Technician		X

Recommendations for Present and Future Roles and Team Membership for Open and Distance Learning Programs and Projects

Many of the roles and competencies listed in the previous examples overlap, blending easily within common groupings. Michael Moore (1993), a recognized authority in the field of open and distance education research who advocates a total systems approach to education and

TABLE 2.5 Building Teams for Open and Distance Learning Environments: Critical Roles and Core Competencies

Critical Role	Core Competencies
Technology expert	Basic knowledge of technology, hardware and multimedia software knowledge and skills, computer networking skills, technology access knowledge, technology transfer knowledge and skills
Instructional designer	Instructional design for interactive technology, needs assessment skills, writing skills, editing skills, graphical design skills
Instructor/program director/administrator	General education theory, distance learning styles and theory, adult learning theory, teaching strategies/models, interpersonal communication, facilitation and feedback skills, presentation skills for open and distance learning, modeling of behavior skills, evaluation skills
Organization change agent	Collaboration and teamwork skills, negotiation skills, group processing skills, change agent skills, public relations skills
Administrator	Support services knowledge, strategic planning skills, organizational skills, marketing skills, managerial skills, budgeting skills, policy-making skills

training, describes open and distance learning environments as settings in which the "instruction is no longer an individual's work, but the work of teams of specialists—media specialists, knowledge specialists, instructional design specialists, and learning specialists" (p. 4). With this team approach in mind, we have synthesized the critical roles and core competencies identified in the previous studies into a matrix (see Table 2.5). This matrix represents our recommendations of how to apply the findings from years of research into a practical working model for designing and implementing programs for open and distance learning environments.

Within this model, the actual instructor is free to focus on content because the production is left to people who are experts at it. These teams are best suited for developing, producing, and evaluating today's and tomorrow's open and distance learning programs and projects (Williams, 1994).

Specialists within the team might include the following:

- Instructor as content expert
- Bilingual communications/assessment specialist
- Instructional designer
- Multimedia support staff
- Computer systems technician
- Training specialist

The team objective would be to assist from the beginning concept phase to the final postproduction evaluation phase to make each educational event, project, and program not only a dynamic production but an effective learning experience. In Chapter 3, you will find a case study complete with detailed descriptions of team member roles, as well as a cost study of what it takes for the team to put together a one-semester college level course.

Preparing Instructors for New Opportunities

SCENARIO

You are preparing instructors for the multimodel distance learning environment. You are concerned about how the technology will affect the learning process.

YOUR TASK

Brainstorm ideas that will help to "engage" remote learners so that even the unassertive learner doesn't "get lost."

DISCUSSION . . .

CHAPTER 3

The Dynamics of the Distance Learning Environment

Chapter 3 offers a broad overview of technical, network, equipment, usage, and cost considerations that can be applied as you set up an open and/or distance learning network.

You will also find several case studies serving as examples of the many ways others have integrated open and distance learning technologies into their learning environments. Case study applications focus on audiographics (telematics), two-way interactive video, personal computer (PC)-based bulletin board, and computer-assisted instruction.

Choosing Appropriate Media

Interconnection Architectures and Protocols

Simply connecting PCs and multimedia workstations through cabling is not nearly enough to create a distance learning network. Each member of the network needs to be able to "shake hands" with all other members of the networks. To shake hands or access one another, the computers/workstations need to speak the same language—that is, have the same interconnection architecture. The interconnection architectures discussed in the following section include open systems interconnections (OSI), transmission control protocol/Internet program (TCP/IP), simple network management protocol (SNMP), and systems network architecture (SNA). Although it is true that with most of today's new equipment these considerations are already seamlessly integrated, it is nontheless valuable to understand what occurs "behind the scenes," in case problems occur.

OSI: Open Systems Interconnection

Developed by the International Standard Organization, OSI is the only internationally accepted framework of standards for communication between two systems made by different vendors. Its goal is to create an open systems networking environment where any vendor's computer system, connected to any other network, can freely share data with any other computer system on that network or a linked network. OSI is a group of layered protocols, or rules for communication. Each of the seven OSI layers performs a specific set of data communications functions, building on the layers below it in the protocol stack. The first three layers of the model are concerned with the local aspect of network computing, or user applications. The next three operate on the network transmission and reception level, and the fourth level essentially acts as an interface between the two (see Table 3.1).

 THE QUESTION:

Why Choose OSI for Your PC-Based Distance Learning Network?

TABLE 3.1 The Seven OSI Layers

1. **Physical layer.** Deals with basic data transfer, physical specifications for connections, bit-level error control, and connection establishment
2. **Data link layer.** Deals with procedures and protocols for operating data links between peer network layer functions; deals with error detection and correction and recovery; adjusts the rate of speed between sending and receiving devices
3. **Network layer.** Determines how data are transferred between computers by identifying network addresses and endpoints; multiplexes data link connections onto several physical link connections; selects between different network services when available; manages error detection, correction, and recovery when service quality cannot be maintained; handles flow and congestion control; provides billing information
4. **Transport layer.** Defines the rules for information exchange between lower and higher layers; selects functions used during data transfer; controls blocking, segmenting, and multiplexing of lower-level connections; controls end-to-end flow control, notification of connection termination, error detection, and error recovery at the data unit level
5. **Session layer.** Concerned with establishing and maintaining sessions between computing entities, normal data exchange, exception reporting, synchronization, session management, and address translation
6. **Presentation layer.** Provides transparent communications services by masking the differences of varying data formats (e.g., character codes establishes session initiation and termination requests, handles data and syntax selection, provides library routines, and provides security encryption)
7. **Application layer.** Contains functions for particular application services such as file transfer, remote file access, and virtual terminals; establishes communication authority and privacy mechanisms; determines cost allocation methods and resource adequacy in light of the necessary grade of service; synchronizes cooperating applications; establishes error recovery responsibilities; identifies data syntax constraints; and maintains agreements on data validity commitment

☞ THE ANSWER:

OSI offers these advantages (Newton, 1991):

- Enhanced synchronicity
- Less expensive network extension devices
- Higher rate of compatibility between devices made by disparate vendors
- More competitive market for interoperable network devices

TCP/IP: Transmission Control Protocol/Internet Program

TCP/IP is a set of protocols developed by the Department of Defense to link dissimilar computers across networks. TCP/IP is an important and established internetworking protocol that works at the third and fourth layers of the OSI model. TCP/IP is designed to be rugged and robust and to guarantee delivery of data in the most demanding circumstances. TCP/IP is popular with networking and computer vendors who want to connect their equipment to a variety of other systems and protocols. It has been implemented on everything from local area networks (LANs) to minis (PCs) to mainframes.

TCP is built on IP:

> TCP provides services
>
> IP gets the data between locations

TCP corresponds with OSI Layers 4 and 5—the transport and sessions layers—having these functions:

- Data transfer support
- Error checking
- Flow control (so that faster, more powerful systems don't control network)
- Status and synchronization control (set up, break, and interrupt connections)

IP has these functions (Newton, 1991, p. 331):

- Tracks Internet address of nodes, routes, and outgoing message
- Recognizes incoming messages, status translation, and communication
- Acts as a gateway to connect networks at OSI network Level 3 and above

SNMP: Simple Network Management Protocol

SNMP came out of the TCP/IP environment. SNMP is the protocol governing network management and monitoring of network devices and their functions. Although SNMP was designed as the TCP stack's network management protocol, it can manage virtually any network type and has been extended to include non-TCP devices (such as 802.1 Ethernet bridges). Although SNMP is widely used in TCP/IP networks, it has also been implemented over Ethernet as well as OSI transports (Newton, 1991, p. 579).

SNA: Systems Network Architecture

SNA is a tree-structured architecture, with a mainframe host computer acting as the network control center. The boundaries described by the host computer—front-end processors, cluster controllers, and desktop terminals—are referred to as the *network's domain*. Unlike OSI and TCP/IP networks, which establish physical paths between terminals for the duration of a session, SNA establishes a logical path between network nodes. SNA then routes each message with addressing information contained in the protocol. The SNA network is, therefore, incompatible with any but approved protocols. It works in several layers, roughly analogous to ISO's seven-level model. However, unlike OSI, SNA is fully defined at each level (Newton, 1991, p. 609).

Network Topologies

A topology is the interconnecting arrangement or configuration of nodes in a telecommunications network. Network topologies can look like anything—from a string with a knot in one end to a plate of spaghetti! These are the most commonly used topologies:

- The star
- The hierarchical tree
- The loop
- The bus
- The ring
- The web

Of these topologies, the three most often used in the world of telecommunications in the 1990s are (a) the bus, (b) the ring, and (c) the star.

Bus Topology

The bus topology is made up of several nodes linked by a common cable, or bus. This is the "string with a knot in the end" topology. The bus is commonly implemented by using coaxial cable and "T" connectors. The failure of any single node on the bus does not cause the network to halt. For example, picture a bus network with a file server at each end of the cable, and 30 nodes strung out in between. Half the nodes are logged into File Server 1, and the other half are logged into File Server 2. If File Server 1 malfunctions for some reason, the nodes logged into it would no longer be able to access its resources. They would, however, be able to log into File Server 2 if they so desired. The failure of any of the 30 workstations on the LAN would have absolutely no effect on the other 29.

The bus topology's major weakness is the bus itself. Any break in the cable will cause the entire network to go down. The first troubleshooting measure to be taken during an unexplained network outage on a bus network is to check all of the cable connections.

Ring Topology

The ring topology is composed of a circular bus, with nodes attached to the ring in much the same manner as the bus topology. As with the bus topology, the failure of one node will not bring down the network. (This is in contrast to "loop" topologies, which make each node a part of the communications path and in which a single machine failure will kill the entire network.)

It is important to realize that the ring spoken of here is not necessarily a large loop of cable. It is possible to implement ring topology networks that look much more like stars than rings. This is because of a piece of equipment called a *concentrator,* or hub. These "black boxes" resemble star networks in that they have several individual cables extending to nodes on the network. Internally, this topology forms a logical ring. In this setup, the hub polls each node in a circular sequence. An actual physical ring becomes apparent only when the installation becomes large enough to require more than one hub. Multiple hubs or concentrators are strung together through "bus in" and "bus out" ports to form the visible ring (Newton, 1991).

Star Topology

The star topology consists of a central hub, connected to several nodes by individual cables. On paper, therefore, the topology can be made to look like a star. This was the logical implementation for many small mainframe and minicomputer installations in the past and has become very popular in the microcomputer world. Its main weakness, the existence of a single "central point of failure," is either planned for in large installations by including redundant systems or tolerated in smaller systems where economy is of primary importance. The inherent reliability of modern PCs and network operating systems is such that catastrophic failures are infrequent.

Transmission Media

Interconnections for telecommunication networks can take many forms: telephone lines, ISDN, coaxial cable, fiber optics, microwave links, infrared links, VSAT (very small aperture terminal) links, BSDN, and ATM.

Telephone Lines

The majority of communication circuits in use are older copper-based conductors. The two major categories are twisted-pair cables and coaxial cables. It's important to begin with these older transmission media, because many people have the misconception that they cannot handle today's telecommunication network demands. Although this is true for applications requiring high bandwidth, the copper-based conductors are quite suitable for many applications.

Twisted Pair (Copper). Twisted pairs are pairs of insulated copper wires, typically 1 millimeter or so in diameter. They are used for almost all local loops. Although the frequency response is normally limited to less than

4khz in the analog portions of telephone networks, they are capable of transmitting frequencies up to the megahertz range over short distances. For purely digital communications, approximately 1.5 MBps is common (twisted pairs are regularly used to transmit T1 and E1 signals), and still-higher rates are occasionally transmitted.

The drawback to using twisted pair is that they can be noisy, especially during electrical storms or when they pass near electrical machinery or other sources of strong electrical interference. This "noise" on the line can interfere with digital transmissions. Although optical fibers are becoming the conductor of choice, twisted pairs will be ubiquitous for many years.

ISDN: Integrated-Services Digital Network

During the 1970s, user demands on telecommunications networks began to include (in addition to voice) the transmission of data, video, video image, text, facsimile, and graphics information. Because these services are not particularly suited to an analog network, an integrated services digital network (ISDN) for universal service began to evolve. ISDN provides end-to-end digital connectivity with access to voice and data services over the same digital transmission. The vision of ISDN has been to

- provide an internationally accepted standard for voice, data, signaling;
- make all transmission circuits end-to-end digital;
- adopt a standard out-of-band signaling system;
- bring significantly more bandwidth to the desktop.

There are 3 basic ISDN services (interfaces) in use today: 2B + D "S," 2B + D "T," and 23B + D (30B + D).

2B + D "S" Interface. The 2B + D is called the basic rate interface (BRI). The "S" interface uses four unshielded normal telephone wires (two twisted-wire pairs) to deliver two "bearer" 64,000 bps channels and one 16,000 bps data-signaling channel. Each of the two 64 KBps bearer or B channels can be used to carry (a) a voice conversation, (b) one high-speed data transmission, or (c) several separate data channels; these channels are multiplexed into one 64 KBps high-speed data line.

2B + D "T." The 2B + D "T" interface delivers the same two 64 KBps bearer channels and one 16 KBps data channel, except that it uses two wires (one pair) and can work at 5 to 10 kilometers.

23B + D or 30B + D. This is called the primary rate interface (PRI). At 23B + D, the channel is 1.5444 MBps. It is the standard T1 line in the United States. The 23B + D operates on two twisted-wire pairs. At 30B + D, the channel is 2.048 MBps. It is the standard E1 line in Europe. The 30B + D also operates on two twisted pairs.

 THE QUESTION:

Why choose ISDN for your PC-based distance learning network?

 THE ANSWER:

ISDN offers these advantages:

- It can integrate several applications (data, voice, fax, video, etc.) simultaneously over one line.
- It runs over plain old telephone (POT) lines (existing twisted pairs).
- It does not require fiber optics.
- It provides clear channel capabilities, so it's not necessary to pay for additional access lines.

Some typical ISDN applications include the following:

- *Simultaneous data calls:* Two end users can talk over the B channel and at the same time exchange information over the D channel.
- *E-mail:* It can carry information to and from unattended phones and PC modems.
- *Collaborative shared-screen capabilities:* Switched data services provided via ISDN lets two remote locations, both equipped with computer/video

terminals, view the same information on their screens and discuss its contents while making changes.

- *Network access:* It allows a person with a PC to gain access to virtually any database on a network (Newton, 1991).

Coaxial Cable

A coaxial cable consists of inner and outer conductors, separated by insulated material. The entire cable is insulated. This construction gives a broad effective bandwidth, up to hundreds of MHz for analog transmission. Digital rates up to 50 MBps for single channels are used on some coaxial cables (baseband transmission) with cumulative transmission rates up to a few hundred MBps when the bandwidth is split up among multiple channels (broadband transmission). Error rates for data transmission in carefully designed systems can be excellent—possibly three orders of magnitude or more below error rates in twisted pairs.

Coaxial cables have been installed in many regions, especially metropolitan areas, as distribution networks for cable TV (CATV) systems, commonly with potential bandwidths on the order of 300 MHz. This gives a large installed base of cables that could be used for high-speed data transmission. In some areas, there are almost as many locations served by CATV as by telephones (Spragins, Hammond, & Pawlikowski, 1991).

Fiber Optics

Fiber optics are increasingly becoming the transmission medium of choice in new installations. Following are some reasons that fiber is used in telecommunication networks.

- Fiber's bandwidth and low error rate (1 bit in 1 trillion) make it suitable for data rates of T1 (E1), T3, and up.
- Fiber is immune to electromagnetic and radio frequency interference (which disturb electrical signals but not light impulses).
- Fiber is secure. Optical transmission emits very little radiation and cannot be tapped without detection because of signal loss through the fiber connection.
- Fiber is easier to install than copper. It is thinner and weighs less.

♦ Fiber is safe in hazardous environments because it is free of electric current.

Fiber has many networking applications:

♦ Connections between workstations and LANs, with cable and repeaters, extend the distance between series of LANs.
♦ Fiber-optic MUXs (multiplexers) and modems provide support for data transmission over a fiber link.
♦ Fiber-optic channel extenders extend mainframe and minicomputer channels to connect remotely located input/output (I/O) devices.
♦ Fiber-optic bridges connect Ethernet or token ring LANs to a fiber network.
♦ Fiber-optic concentrators support multiple workstations on a fiber network and interconnect fiber networks.

Microwave Links: Short-Haul Radio

The advancement in radio manufacturing technology over the years, and the allocation of the 10-, 18-, and 23-GHz radio spectrums for point-to-point microwave use have made short-haul radios especially reliable and cost-effective for some telecommunication network applications. The majority of these radios are digital, and they transport both voice and data under the telephony digital hierarchy formats of T1, T2, and T3 transmission speeds.

A short-haul radio system is composed of one or more links of terrestrial radios, transmitting and receiving at very high frequencies in the GHz range. A radio modulates an incoming T1 signal consisting of both voice and data traffic and transmits to the distant end. Both analog voice circuits and digital data lines are modulated up to the T1 speed by means of a channel bank or T1 multiplexer. A network can then be established by setting up one or more pairs of radios (with each pair of radios having direct line of site).

A short-haul radio system is economical, highly efficient, and reliable; it gives the user direct control over the network. Some of the applications of short-haul radio systems include the following:

♦ To establish a data and voice network that links multiple LANs together through T1 gateways or a 10-MBps LAN bridge

- To provide a bypass direct-access link to the long-distance carrier, thereby eliminating special-access charges
- To provide a disaster control alternative

Unlike telephone line and fiber-optic transmission media, terrestrial microwave does not require securing right-of-way. In addition, microwave transmissions will not suffer long outages due to cable breaks and the like, and they are easier and less expensive to install (Wang, 1990).

Infrared Links

Atmospheric infrared transmission is a short-range alternative to transmission by microwave, satellite, fiber, or copper. Commercially available since the 1960s, infrared transmitters emit a directional, highly coherent beam of electromagnetic energy, typically in the 830 mm wavelength range. This frequency of electromagnetic energy attenuates rapidly in the earth's atmosphere, giving it a limited range (10 miles under ideal conditions). Because of its quick attenuation and lack of interference with the microwave spectrum, the Federal Aviation Administration (FAA) does not require licensing of infrared installations. This simplifies their construction, because no license, permit, or right-of-way are required. The technology is capable of delivering data rates as high as DS3 over a limited range under almost any weather conditions, making it a serious contender for interbuilding LAN interconnection. If right-of-way is difficult or impossible to obtain and distances are relatively short, infrared can pay for itself in as little as 1 year when compared with the cost of using telephone company provided T- or E-carrier facilities.

Infrared is also a viable contender with fiber in applications involving electronically hostile environments. Indoors or out, it can provide high-speed data communications in situations in which physical cable is a disadvantage. Under good conditions, infrared transmissions can provide bit error rates on the order of 10–8 to 10–9. Any phenomena, however, that affects normal vision will have some effect on the bit error rate (BER) of infrared. Although not as susceptible to rain, fog, and snow as once thought, this technology can be affected by high winds and high temperatures. Winds affect infrared signals by introducing more particles of dust and grit into the atmosphere, interfering with the infrared beam and introducing errors into the signal. This phenomenon

Dynamics of the Distance Learning Environment 47

is called *scattering*. A second problem, *shimmer*, is caused by variation in air temperature. These heat waves cause variations in air density, refracting some of the infrared energy out of its intended path and introducing errors into the signal.

Despite these problems, the ability to operate infrared equipment without fear of interference from microwave transmissions is a strong advantage in environments where the electromagnetic spectrum is very cluttered (Minoli, 1990).

VSAT Links

VSAT (very small aperture terminal) networks are emerging as a popular distance learning telecommunications solution because of their ability to provide affordable, high-quality data, voice, and video communications. This is especially important to organizations driven by cost, performance, and lack-of-access factors.

> You can go to http://www.supcom.com/vsat.htm to learn how large companies such as Scientific Atlanta Network Group, Avdata, GE Spacenet, Data Transmission Network, Farm Data, Wescott Communications, AT&T Tridom, Motion Industries, and many others are deploying VSAT networks.

Following are some of the features of VSATs:

- They provide the technology to efficiently connect remote LANs by offering digital connectivity to all network sites.
- They supply bandwidth to each site on demand.
- They provide optimum solution for "bursty" LAN traffic.
- They offer efficient broadcast capabilities for repetitive information (database update applications, compressed video applications).

Typically, in a star topology, with the hub station ranging in size from 6 to 9 meters, a VSAT network usually supports two-way transmission between numerous remote locations. It is common for twenty or more remote data centers to connect to such a network, with remote VSAT terminals using small .75- to 1.8-meter antennae. These antennae are connected to the users' processing equipment by antenna-mounted radio frequency electronics and an indoor digital interface unit.

> VSAT can be used for applications that include LANs, minicomputers, mainframes, PCs, voice, asynchronous terminals, compressed video.

VSATs typically receive data at rates of 128 to 512 KBps and transmit data at rates of 63 KBps to T1 (E1). The limiting factor is cost related. Wider bandwidth transmissions require leasing or purchasing multiple satellite channels.

BISDN: Broadband Integrated Services Digital Network

BISDN meets the need for services requiring bit rates greater than 2 megabytes. Access can be based on a single optical fiber. BISDN's biggest advantage is *bandwidth on demand*. Some of the applications for BISDN include (a) broadband video, (b) high-speed unrestricted digital information transmission, (c) high-speed file transfer, and (d) high-speed, high-resolution facsimile, color facsimile, and video/document retrieval.

In the United States, pressure has arisen on BISDN standards because of the need to interconnect remote LANs. Characteristics of the BISDN standard include (a) handling both narrowband and broadband rates, (b) handling both continuous and bursty traffic, (c) satisfying delay- and/or loss-sensitive quality requirements, and (d) meeting future unforeseen needs (Minoli, 1993).

ATM: Asynchronous Transfer Mode

ATM is a high bandwidth, low-delay packetlike switching and multiplexing technique. Usable capacity is segmented into fixed-size cells, consisting of header and information fields, allocated to services on demand. The CCITT (Comité Consulatif International Téléphonique et Télégraphique) has selected ATM as the transport structure for broadband communication network because of its flexibility and suitability for both transmission and switching. ATM is a connection-oriented process, although it is designed as a basis for supporting both connectionless and connection-oriented services. ATM deals with procedures for allocating bandwidth at the user interface and allocating the bandwidth to various user services. ATM is similar to packet switching but with the following differences:

- Protocols are simplified—no error control of information field and no flow controls on the links.
- Cells (packets) have a fixed and small length (no variable cells allowed). This framework allows very high-speed switching nodes, because the logical decisions are straightforward.
- The header provides only limited Layer 2 functionality. ATM does not incorporate higher-layer functionality. As a result, information transfer can be accomplished faster.

ATM has begun to penetrate next-generation telecommunications networks at the core as a standard technology. Appropriate ATM-based telecommunications equipment is under development to support a variety of new applications:

- Desk-to-desk video conferencing
- Multimedia conferencing
- Multimedia messaging
- Interactive digital video for distance learning
- Imaging tasks (computer-aided design—CAD/CAM)
- Animation, simulation
- Data fusion
- Collaborative work environments
- Supercomputer access

These applications are all characterized by very high bandwidth requirements. ATM can deliver such bandwidth to the desktop and across LANs and wide area networks (WANs).

Emerging High-Speed Services and Applications

As the number of applications requiring high-speed data networking increases, so does the need for higher data transmission rates. In addition to the transmission mediums we have discussed, another service application beginning to emerge is Internet provider (IP)-based videoconferencing.

IP-based videoconferencing to the PC desktop enables videoconferencing to be moved over LANs and WANs along with data transfer and sharing. Part of what drives IP videoconferencing is the trend for PC vendors to bundle video software with desktops. It is projected that by the end of 1998, PCs will automatically be shipped with cameras and videoconferencing software. Another reason for the excitement about IP video is its potential to seamlessly link businesses with clients, universities with students, without the need for expensive point-to-point, proprietary equipment. Technically, anyone anywhere with a PC can use the Internet to visually meet with colleagues around the globe—for the cost of a local phone call. At the time of this writing (mid-1998), the problem with IP videoconferencing has been its reliability and manageability on the network. Reliability in video quality is not yet consistent, because of the way data packets are transferred over the Internet; video requires that large packets be routed and delivered together. Manageability of bandwidth for LANs and WANs is a problem because of the potential bandwidth bottlenecks it can cause. The International Telecommunications Union's Standards Committee has been working on revising the H.323 protocol to address these and other concerns about video over the Internet. The latest revision to the H.323 specification is nicknamed "h.mediamiv"—a series of management information databases for all networking video equipment. This standard is critical because it will define how these various vendor products can be managed via SNMP. Once this happens, IP videoconferencing will move out of the category of "emerging technologies" and into the mainstream of videoconferencing. (*PC Magazine* writer Stephanie Neil, 1998, estimates that will happen around the year 2000.)

Putting It All Together: Choosing Open and Distance Learning Technologies That Fit the Application

The integration of telecommunications systems into an institution is often driven by the kinds of backbone technical capabilities we've been discussing. Table 3.2 provides further insight into the variety of telecommunications technologies available for open and distance learning. We hope that the information in this section will help you to better understand the choices available and help form the basis you need to tailor a telecommunications solution for your specific application. We strongly suggest that the implementation of any telecommunications plan be preceded by (a) an environmental scan that determines which form of telecommunications is right for the organization; (b) an assessment of the types of programs that fit within the institution's mission, resources, and goals; (c) an understanding of learner attributes and needs; and (d) the development of instructional design processes that integrate the attributes of the technology with the attributes and needs of the institution and the learners.

Applications for Distance Learning

Table 3.2 was designed to help you better understand the commonality and variations among the components of the various telecommunications systems. Included were examples of approximate start-up costs. There will also be ongoing costs associated with things such as (a) additional personnel needed for technical, training, and administrative support; (b) time and resources invested in faculty development; and (c) increased development time for programs and materials.

This next section contains two case studies with detailed descriptions of the kinds of material and people resources needed, as well as developmental costing worksheets. The first case study, titled "A Just-in-Time Team Approach to Faculty Development," describes faculty and materials development for a two-way interactive video course. The second case study is "Using Audiographics (Telematics), Electronic Bulletin Board (Intranet/Internet/Extranet), and Computer-Assisted Instruction to Certify Rural Emergency Medical Technicians Through a Regional Educational Outreach Network."

These examples have been included to get you thinking about your institution's transition to open and distance learning. Although your institutional environmental scan will uncover a unique set of resources and needs, these examples will help you form the questions you'll need to ask as you get started.

TABLE 3.2 Open and Distance Learning Technologies[a]

	Voice Teleconferencing	Audiographics (Telematics)	PC-Based On-Line Internet and World Wide Web
Method	Two or more sites connected in teleconference • Everyone hears all • Handouts by mail/FAX	Multiple sites connected via computer Everyone hears, interacts with everyone else through graphic information transmitted via computer over plain old telephone service (POTS)	Multiple sites connected via computer • Option of synchronous or asynchronous activities • Work/study "on demand"
Equipment	• Telephones or speaker systems • Digital conference bridge	• Telephones, PCs, speaker system, modems (2—high speed and low speed), graphics tablet, camcorder, printer	Multimedia PCs, modems, peripheral hardware as desired (camcorders, printers, scanners, network cards, etc.), peripheral software as desired (See-Me, See-You, Pro-Share)
Costs (approximate as of 1996; may differ by geography or company)	• Digital bridge, $4,000 per port • Conferencing system $1,500 • Long distance charges	• PC, peripherals including targa board and TeleMedicine software, modems (> $6,000) • High speed modem, $150 • 20" video monitor, $1,000 • Conferencing system $1,500 • Option: "Buy" air time, about 27 cents per minute, per site • Digital bridge, $4,000 per port • Long distance charges • Option: "Buy" airtime, about 27 cents per minute, per site • Camcorder, $1,500 • Printer, $500	$3,200 to $4,500, depending on hardware/software options
Advantages	• Real-time voice communications • Equipment and operations are easy to use • Moderate capital investment	• Use POTS • Can use one phone line only • Real-time voice/date communication • Special interest packages allow high-quality screen capture for specialized applications	• Easy, cost-effective way to get started in distance education • Most students already "computer literate"
Disadvantages	• No video • High telephone line charges	• No live video of instructor • Specialty applications need 2 POTS • Many older, rural telephone lines are full of static that can compromise connection integrity	• Depending on application, may need high capacity telephone lines

	One-Way Satellite	Compressed Video	Full-Motion Video
Method	• High-quality video of instructor and distant class • Variety of programming	• Two or more sites connected with interactive video/audio • Instructor sees and hears students • Students see and hear instructor and other students at other sites • Multiple cameras transmit graphics, visual aids, multiple room shots	• Two or more sites connect into two-way, full-motion audio/video teleconference • Instructor sees and hears all • Students see and hear all • Multiple cameras transmit graphics, visual aids, multiple room shots
Equipment	• Easy to use • TV monitors, satellite/microwave/cable, hookup/telephones	• CODECs (coder-decoders), monitors, computer, cameras, graphics tablet, FAX, microphones, printers, scanners • VSAT: Satellite dishes/transponders/receivers • Fiber: T1-T3 lines • ISDN: BRIs or PRIs	• Video CODECs for transmission/reception, monitors, dedicated fiber plant
Costs (approximate as of 1996; may differ by geography or company)	• $1,000 to $10,000 for satellite downlinks • Subscription fees from $2,000 to $10,000 • Special programs extra • Cable installation from $18,000 to $25,000/mile (less than $10,000 for receiving sites)	• $60,000 to $80,000 per site—full-room systems • $6,000 to $15,000 desktop PC units • VSAT: Subscription fees ($2,000-$10,000); cost per hour, about $50.00 • T1 or fractional T1: Nonrecurring installation and connection charges; recurring charges in the range of $1,000 per month • ISDN: BRIs or PRIs; recurring monthly charge ($60-$90 per 112 KBp line, plus per-minute usage charge); dial up (pay per call) also an option	• $10,000 to $50,000 for coders/decoders, monitors, microphones per site • Lease/purchase an option • Costs dropping • Promise of "information highway" • Fiber installation plus usage • Line costs about $30 to $70/mile/month
Advantages	• High-quality video • Variety of courses • Easy to use • Satellites not restricted by geography	• Near real-time voice/graphic/audio communication • Everyone sees/hears everyone • Easy to use • Local control • Quality fine for continuing education	• Real-time, high-quality video/graphic/audio communication • Everyone sees/hears all • Local control • Easy interaction
Disadvantages	• Maintenance may or may not be included • May be unable to interact with instructor without special WATTS lines • Curricula and scheduling decided by provider • No local control • Two-way video not an option	• High start-up costs • Need supporting infrastructure (engineering, ID, etc.) • Quality may not be sufficient for some applications (telemed) • Fractional high-speed lines not always available (last mile delivery)	• High quality • Cost for network facilities may be prohibitive • Need support infrastructure • Fiber not available everywhere (last mile delivery)

a. Prices are subject to change. For current pricing, contact local/national representatives. Prices represented in U.S. dollars.

54   DISTANCE LEARNING

✎ CASE STUDY 1: INTRODUCTORY INFORMATION

A Just-in-Time Team Approach to Faculty Development

An ideal approach to supporting a multimodel distance learning project is the "Just-in-Time/Just Enough" team approach (Williams, 1994). In this model, the instructor acts as the content expert and has a team of people who will take care of the many details involved as they come up—that is, "just-in-time." Also, the instructor is not overwhelmed with having to think about reformatting an entire course at once. Instead, the materials and course conversion are done in increments—that is, "just enough." This approach takes a dedicated team, whose existence is supported by project managers and who will not be pulled off the project. A description of the multimodel support team members follows, along with a listing of their roles and responsibilities:

The Planning, Design, and Implementation Team Members

- Instructor as content expert
- Bilingual communications/assessment specialist
- Faculty/instructor intermediary
- Instructional designer
- Multimedia support staff
- Computer systems technician
- Training specialist

Instructor as Content Expert. In this study, the instructors were literally "teaching" their peers, because both groups—instructors and students—were physicians. The difference between the two groups was that the instructors practiced in a fast-paced, urban tertiary-care environment and the students at the remote site practiced in a slower-paced rural clinic setting. The instructors, therefore, were perceived to be highly specialized, cutting-edge clinicians from whom the rural physicians could learn the latest medical techniques and developments that would help them in their respective practices. The instructors were familiar with their audience and could anticipate potential student needs, responses, and expectations. The goal, therefore, was to employ a total systems approach to faculty development in which the instructor was free to concentrate on his or her content specialization, leaving the work of designing the instruction and the materials to the specialty team.

Bilingual Communications/Assessment Specialist. The communications specialist is the first team member the content expert encounters. In this study, it was found that the communications specialist needed to be articulate, precise, and knowledgeable regarding distance education technologies and environments and to be perceived as alert, analytical, and capable. These qualities were important to gain the instructors' trust, and to belie an unspoken yet very real sense of skepticism concerning the team's ability to understand the medical materials well enough to successfully follow through. In this initial encounter, therefore, important qualities of the communications specialist included the ability to grasp the main ideas of the content presented and to verbalize how the advantages and limitations of distance education technologies affected presentation of that content.

Instructional Design Specialist. The role of the instruction designer is to reengineer the materials used in the traditional classroom to fit the visual/computer-based/multimedia distance education environment. Important qualities of this individual were found to be the ability to combine two seemingly opposed processes—structural planning and unstructured creative thinking. Structured planning is needed for organizing, sequencing, and integrating the lesson components to produce a clear, concise presentation that is easily followed and understood. Unstructured free flow of ideas and expressions—creative thinking—is needed to find solutions to problems that arise during planning.

Training Specialist. In this study, the training specialist introduced the instructors to the distance education environment: the production-like room complete with cameras, lighting, microphones, and a variety of peripherals. Techniques for managing limitations of the technology were discussed. Some of these limitations include the loss of eye contact, difficulty reading body language, and loss of immediate feedback associated with audio and video delays inherent in teaching from a distance. In addition, learning strategies of chunking (described later), advanced organizers, and sequencing were introduced.

"Practice" was emphasized as the key to feeling comfortable with the distance learning environment and getting past the perceived limitations of the technological environment. The importance of becoming familiar with timing and transitions as well as interacting with cameras and other peripheral equipment was stressed.

Multimedia Support Staff. These individuals met with and assisted the instructors in preparing and refining courseware materials. The preferred action was to transport materials to an electronic digital presentation format that served as the framework on which the class from a distance was built. During the course of this study, the researcher found using such a framework to be the simplest method of engaging instructors in teaching from a distance. With all materials prepared in advance and downloaded to the computer running the interactive video conference, the instructor was freed from the bother of collecting, organizing, and bringing the materials needed for practice sessions and the actual presentation. In many cases, this simple action on the part of the multimedia specialists made the already preoccupied instructors more willing to attempt teaching from a distance, because all necessary materials were so readily accessed.

Computer Systems Technician. This individual was responsible for integrating peripheral electronic teaching aids (e.g., the video microscope) into the presentation. A "seamless" quality of presentation—that is, enabling the technology concerns to drop to the background—is absolutely dependent on the knowledge, skills, and creativity of this hardware specialist (Williams, 1994).

✎ CASE STUDY 1

A Just-in-Time Team Approach to Faculty Development

In this case study, the decision was made to take a "just-in-time" team approach for faculty development rather than send faculty to a one- or two-day workshop. The team of specialists described interfaced with the instructor in a total systems approach to the design, development, and presentation of a 1-hour continuing medical education class taught. Many of the skills and competencies as well as responsibilities of the design team overlap. In this model, where resources are limited, one person can "wear many hats." In the following description, the reader will be able to draw from his or her own experiences and formulate a systems approach that will fit his or her resources and environment.

As previously explained, the communications specialist had the first contact with the instructor. Because all appointments were scheduled during clinic hours, the design team was advised that no more than 30 minutes per meeting would be possible. The initial 30-minute visit was structured to introduce the instructor to the concept of teaching from a distance, while at the same time collecting materials needed for the presentation. In some cases, the variety of materials desired to create an effective, interesting visual production were readily available to the communications specialist (photographs, drawings, video clips). In other instances, it was important to provide the instructor with a vision of how external materials enhance teaching in the visual environment of two-way interactive video.

In this study, the task was accomplished by obtaining a copy of the lecture materials for review and asking for a second 30-minute appointment to clarify the flow of the events of instruction. Once consensus was reached between the communications specialist and the instructor, an appointment was scheduled with the instructional design specialist.

Instructional design considerations discussed included planning content in a design that would at one time organize and "frame" the presentation from a distance—maximize student interaction—and organize and prepare graphics to fit the visual format. "Chunking"—a presentation strategy used by many adult educators to break the traditional 50-minute lecture into shorter segments that encourage student interaction—was introduced to instructors. Some of the more common chunking strategies include small-group reports, case study presentations, and planned question-and-answer sessions. The purpose of weaving these interactive strategies into the instructional design was to make the class from a distance as relevant and interesting as possible. Because research has shown that students can easily get distracted in classes taught from a distance, every effort was made to mentally, emotionally, and psychologically "pull" each student into the activity of the class. Strategies intentionally avoided long periods of time when instructors appeared only as a "talking head" or when students were subjected to "talking slides," seeing only a series of static slides with the instructor's voice in the background.

The conceptual reengineering of the lecture materials by the instructional designer was then reviewed with the instructor at the next 30-minute appointment. At this meeting, both the communications and instructional design specialists met with the instructor. The instructor was gently prodded regarding the possibility of integrating visual aids into the production; if this was amenable, the communications specialist offered to take care of all materials reproduction concerns (in many cases, the researcher found that instructors simply could not find time to gather and organize visual materials because of their heavy clinical patient loads).

Next, a 30-minute meeting was scheduled to meet with the creative production specialist and the technical production specialist in the digital imaging lab to review changes that had been made to prepare the instructor's original materials for the compressed video environment. It was explained to instructors that television graphics and multimedia presentations require different visual enhancements than static overhead slides. Instructors were told the importance of keeping presentation materials simple: The audience at a distance cannot see or understand complicated graphics and text screens that may be acceptable in a face-to-face situation in the form of slide presentations. When the audience cannot see or understand visuals and there is no instructor physically present to focus their attention, students may lose interest and the message may be lost. Adjustments and additions that fit within the guidelines presented were then made to the presentation. An additional 30-minute session with the creative specialist was scheduled for final approval of materials.

A 30-minute appointment followed with the training specialist. For this initial meeting, a satellite connection was established with the remote site, and the system was configured in a "loop-back" mode. In loop-back, the video and audio signals were sent to the satellite transponder and then returned to the monitor in the teaching room, simulating for the instructors what both they and the students at the remote site would be experiencing. In this way, the instructor could experience what teaching from a distance would actually be like. The rehearsal also provided the opportunity for instructors to get past the "first-time jitters" of viewing oneself on television, to pace instruction to fit within the time restraints, to develop a comfort level with the environment that, ideally, would result in a relaxed flow of activity, and to focus on the remote audience rather than on the technology or the content.

During this working session, the instructor was able to get "hands-on" experience working with the technologies. Special attention was given to coaching the instructors on developing a comfort level with the new environment, to reinforcing existing presentation skills, and to cultivating the new skills of working with cameras and peripherals. Instructors were guided and coached through unfamiliar experiences such as looking at and talking to cameras and speaking into the microphones.

All instructors appeared to enjoy the experience, finding the technology easy to use and nonthreatening. Most thought a second and third practice session were not necessary. However, all instructors agreed to return for at least one 30-minute practice session.

The purpose of the second session was to allow the trainer to see the instructor in action and to provide appropriate feedback. Once accomplished, instructors were then left alone to practice. Videotapes were provided for each instructor to record the presentation. The purpose of the tape was to provide the instructors a self-evaluation tool for reviewing their teaching style, presentation skills, and personal habits.

Tapings were done in private, with the trainer on-call to answer questions or solve technical problems. Students were not included in any practice sessions. Instructors were encouraged, but not required, to practice again before the actual presentation (Williams, 1994).

Team Objective

The overall objective of the "Just-in-Time/Just Enough" approach is to guarantee an effective learning experience for both instructors and learners. Although the approach is time-consuming initially, it saves time in the long run: Models built early on are replicated, and reformatted materials are easy to update and manipulate in their new format.

✐ $$ COST FACTORS $$

Additional Personnel Needed for the Just-in-Time Team Approach to Faculty Development

Table 3.3 shows the number of people needed to maintain video-based distance learning in Case Study 1. Cost figures were calculated by averaging the hourly rate of participants involved in preparing and delivering instruction from a distance. (You'll need to calculate average salary per hour using your own local hourly rates.) The example is based on developing and producing 8 contact hours of instruction (Williams, Smith, & Myers, 1995).

TABLE 3.3

Total Number of Support Personnel	Average Hours Spent Per Class (8 contact hours of instruction) Average Salary[a]: $15.00 Per Hour Formula: 7 Personnel × 8 Hours Instruction × $15.00 Per Hour	
Instructor as content expert	4 hrs.	
Communications specialist	4 hrs.	8 personnel × 47 hrs. (total) × $15.00 per hr. = $5,640.00 to develop and produce 8 hours of instruction
Instructional designer	12 hrs.	
Multimedia support staff	28 hrs.	
Computer systems technician	1 hr.	
Training specialist	2 hrs.	

a. Calculate average salary per hour using your own local hourly rates.

CASE STUDY 2: INTRODUCTORY INFORMATION

What Is Audiographics (Telematics) and How Is It Used for Distance Learning?

Audiographics provides users with the capability to interact with one another through two-way voice and graphic communication and to share images simultaneously on high-resolution color monitors. This is done by combining PC computers with modems and POTS (plain old telephone service), with solid instructional design principles. Audiographic systems offer multimedia presentation capability for the preparation and delivery of subject matter. The multimedia features include an electronic blackboard, PC-generated graphics/text, and still-frame video. Course materials are captured from PC paint/graphics packages, and video sources are stored, transmitted, recalled, and annotated from any station in real time.

The result: a cost-effective distance learning delivery method.

Appeal of Audiographics (Telematics)

Audiographic systems offer the following advantages:

- Transmission costs are comparatively inexpensive.
- Equipment is comparatively inexpensive.
- They are easy to use, requiring little or no familiarity with PCS.
- They are easy to install—can be installed almost anywhere there is standard telephone service.
- They provide new distance learning programs the ability to start small—within existing budgets and capabilities—and expand in outreach as resources and levels of experience increase.
- Systems can easily be configured for point-to-point or multipoint applications.

CASE STUDY 2: INTRODUCTORY INFORMATION

What Is a BBS and How Is It Used for On-Line Distance Learning?

Bulletin Board System (BBS) is a fancy name for an electronic message system running on a microcomputer. The system is like a physical bulletin board except that BBS messages are posted electronically. A BBS allows features such as the following:

- ❖ Screen sharing: Students at different sites can collaborate on the same shared-screen space.
- ❖ Instruction and activity can be originated from any site.
- ❖ Students can access and incorporate the Internet before, during, and after class.
- ❖ Students can access the BBS at anytime, day or night, from home or work.

Because of technological advances, BBSs have evolved rapidly over the past few years to include Intranet (local area network), Internet (global network), and Extranet (local area network privileges extend to home PC) capabilities. The most widely used BBS application is computer messaging, or electronic mail (e-mail). Other BBS applications include computer-mediated conferencing (CMC) and computer-assisted instruction (CAI).

Electronic Mail (E-Mail). This computer messaging application allows students to leave messages for the instructor and for fellow students at remote sites. It is a noninteractive application (asynchronous), meaning that the sending party does not enter into a real-time dialogue with the recipients. Messages are left for recipients to get when convenient.

Computer-Mediated Conferencing (CMC). This is a sophisticated variation of e-mail. CMC supports communication within groups. It is an interactive application (synchronous), meaning that an unlimited number of students can all "join" a conference at the same time and "chat" on-line with each other about an area of concern, an upcoming test, or a special project. CMC participants can also store "conversations" as messages on the computer for later retrieval.

Computer-Assisted Instruction (CAI). Through the bulletin board, students can "download" supplementary training programs to use as study modules along with the topics on the syllabus.

🖉 CASE STUDY 2: INTRODUCTORY INFORMATION

Getting a BBS Started

Technically, a BBS can be set up on any PC with any communications software and virtually any baud modem. Getting a BBS equipped with applications that fit the perceived needs of the target audience takes research and planning. Questions to consider include these: How do I want to use this BBS? Who is my audience? What applications and features will be offered? Who will be responsible for telephone access time? Will I charge a fee or offer the BBS as a free service? Who will maintain the BBS? The answers to these questions will decide what choices one makes regarding (a) telephone line access, (b) hardware, (c) system operators (SYSOPS), and (d) software.

Telephone Line Access. You can run a single-line BBS over an existing telephone line. A dedicated access line providing 24-hour uninterrupted service is better. In the United States, the cost for installing an additional line as a hobby is today about $100.00, with monthly charges ranging from $19.00 to $27.00, depending on the telephone company and electives. However, if users pay access fees, you will need to install a business line. Installation charges for a business line vary widely but can average around $250.00, with monthly charges of approximately $50.00. For multiple-line BBSs, decisions must also be made about installing roll-over lines.

Hardware. Hardware selection depends on how you plan to use the BBS. A basic Level 1 line system can operate off a pre-Pentium-generation PC. A multiline system requires a Pentium or Pentium II computer with enough megabytes of RAM and a large enough hard disk drive to support your software. You will also need a modem for each line coming into the system. A 56K modem is recommended. Modem choice is a matter of cost, demand, and application. Whichever speed you choose, you will need to make sure the modem is completely compatible with the software you use. If it is not, you may run into connectivity problems. Fortunately, advanced software operating systems like Windows '95 and '98 are intuitive, automatically checking for and configuring modem/PC for compatibility.

SYSOPs (System Operators). Depending on user activity, running a BBS can take from 1 to 8 hours a day to answer e-mail and keep the BBS running smoothly. "Housekeeping" chores also take time (backing up the system's files; updating user databases, program offerings, and bulletins; adding new features; searching public domain software and shareware to keep the BBS current; installing software updates; and dealing with the inevitable hardware "crashes"). Decisions also need to be made about duties of SYSOPs. What will it take for the system to run efficiently and smoothly? One system operator or several?

Software. The range in BBS Software prices and capabilities is wide. You'll find everything from single-line shareware you can download from existing BBSs for no cost to expensive multiline systems costing hundreds of dollars. Most of the major BBS vendors have demo disks that let you simulate a BBS environment. Typically, these demos will allow your computer to function as a point-to-point messaging BBS (i.e., you can send/receive e-mail). Other features and options are not accessible. Demo disks make it easy to see if the software (a) fits your applications, (b) is user friendly, and (c) is compatible with your hardware. The demo disks also make it possible to show what a BBS can do, instead of just talking about its capabilities.

CASE STUDY 2: INTRODUCTORY INFORMATION

*A Few Questions to Think About When
Designing a Communications Network*

1. What educational and administrative members will need access?
2. What line capacity and modem speeds are indicated by applications?
3. How many users? At host site? Remote sites?
4. Anticipated flow of traffic? How many telephone lines indicated?
5. Will existing networks be tied in? How will they be interfaced?
6. What applications? E-mail? File transfer? Computer conferencing?
7. What bandwidth needs? Will standard analog lines fit applications?
8. How many sites will be able to have simultaneous access to the host?

Introducing Telecommunications Networking to Rural Sites

1. Introduce the concept of a telecommunications network.
2. Discover the degree of interest in proposed network.
3. Talk through telecommunication options to help remote administrators determine if either administrative or educational needs exist at their facility.
4. Find out how these needs are being addressed in current environment.
5. Physically demonstrate the bulletin board system (BBS) with hands-on e-mail, interactive "chatting" demonstration (laptop computer demo).
6. Provide information on start-up and maintenance costs.
7. Provide options for obtaining needed funding.
8. Assist in grant writing, if interest exists.
9. Determine the capabilities of the existing PBX network; make technical recommendations where necessary.

Selecting Hardware and Software

In the case study, the key to hardware and software choices at both local and remote sites was talking to the end users about the applications needed and the amount of on-line time the applications will take. (Based on the field assessment, three options for connectivity and hardware selections were given for implementing the BBS.)

✎ CASE STUDY 2

Using Audiographics (Telematics), Electronic Bulletin Board (Intranet/Internet/Extranet), and Computer-Assisted Instruction to Certify Rural Emergency Medical Technicians Through a Regional Educational Outreach Network

History and Background

In the United States, there is a growing concern over the adequacy of health care services—preventive, emergency, continuing education, consultation—in rural communities. Rural areas have been particularly hard hit by the demise of many rural community hospitals and clinics. These rural areas do not have the resources to access the health care services that directly affect the quality of life of people in the community. One large midwestern tertiary-care facility piloted a distance learning model network project. The purpose of the model project was to make it possible for rural sites to access information, services, training, and support using standard analog telephone lines. The system uses shared-screen audiographics as the mode of instruction and bulletin board applications (e-mail, computer-managed conferencing, computer-aided instruction [CAI] file transfer) as the support system. The project began as a way to bring recertification courses to paramedics and emergency medical personnel.

Getting the Audiographics Stations Started

"Workstations" were installed at ambulance and/or fire house stations. Each workstation consisted of a PC, speaker telephone system modem, graphics writing tablet, switch box to access two modems (low speed for the class; high speed for e-mail and Internet activities), and an audiocassette system. Using this system, students met electronically for classes and interacted with the instructor and with students at other sites during each lesson.

With this setup, students remained in their hometowns on duty in case they were needed on a fire or ambulance run.

The Class

Two rural emergency medical technician (EMT)/intermediate sites connected with the instructor at the tertiary-care center in central Texas. One site had four students; the other site had nine students. Instructional design strategies were built around the content, the task at hand, the attributes of the learners, the teacher, and the technology.

Class Notes

Sometimes, students were instructed to follow along with the lecture. Other times, students broke up into groups to discuss medical protocols, then used the electronic pen on the graphic tablet to write answers on the screen. The answers could be viewed by the instructor and the students at the other sites; students then used the speaker telephones to discuss answer rationales. For skills training, instructors or preceptors traveled to the remote or students traveled to the tertiary-care facility.

All of the computer screens for the course were preloaded onto the computers; therefore, students who wanted to view the screens again could easily do so when they were studying for tests.

In addition, CAI modules specific to the class materials were designed and loaded onto the computers for students to take practice tests and remedial training. Students with computers were given CAI disks for home study and review. A computerized BBS was established for students to use electronic mail software to type questions 24 hours a day to the instructors. Each day, instructors reviewed their electronic mail (e-mail) and responded to the individual needs of the learner by sending a personalized message back to the student on the BBS.

The Bottom Line

Audiographics solved the problem of who provides coverage when everyone is off to classes in the big cities. Students also saved money on tuition, which was reduced because there was no face-to-face instructor, gasoline, food, and lost wages due to the down time of traveling 100+ miles to take the class.

Comments From the Field

"While the students did not see an instructor during the training, they were surrounded by more learning resources than most class instruction typically offers. The audiographic network is geared toward providing resources so that students who cannot grasp the material fast can access additional information and experience individualized tutorial training. . . . We were very pleased with the results of the first course, and all of the students did exceptionally well academically. . . . The students were very enthusiastic about this new distance learning technology and were wonderful, interactive students who really seemed to enjoy taking the course inside their ambulance stations without having to make long drives to urban training sites." (Program Director)

"The number of topics that can be taught on this system is limited only by the imagination. We anticipate adding nursing training, respiratory therapy training, medical technical training, EMS management, OSHA awareness. We will also be adding grief counseling courses through our clinical pastoral program very soon. This audiographics network has the potential to transform the rural ambulance station and/or hospital into a unique health education center for rural learners, thereby greatly enhancing the public relations value of our hospital." (Dean of Education)

"The audiographics network is considerably less expensive to install and operate then other distance learning technologies. This is important, because rural communities cannot afford fiber-optic lines for two-way interactive videoconferencing or down linking equipment for satellite communication." (Telecommunications Network Director)

Getting the Bulletin Board System (BBS) Started

Because of the effectiveness of the audiographics installation, we were asked by outlying clinics and hospitals to extend the project to their rural sites. Eight sites were selected. From the needs assessments conducted at each site, these immediate needs were identified:

1. An educational link for nurses, paraprofessionals, other hospital and clinic staff members
2. A vehicle for physician consultation and patient file transfer
3. A communication link for rural administrators

Based on this needs assessment, BBS planning and development began. The number of simultaneous users was estimated to be low. The eight health care facilities averaged 35 beds, with 6 to 12 physicians. Several BBS software packages were researched. Packages ranged in capability from allowing access from one person to hundreds of persons. Packages that allowed access for one to four users simultaneously were the most cost-effective. Above four users, the prices for hardware and software jumped considerably. Therefore, because of the anticipated low volume of traffic and the budgetary constraints of the pilot project, a four-line roll-over configuration was chosen for the model network.

The next step was to assess local (host) and remote site resources and facilities.

Local (Host) Site Analysis

The existing telecommunications facilities of the tertiary-care center's Novell network was determined to be adequate to support the project. The decision was made, however, to keep the model network based on these technical and application considerations:

1. *Technical.* The network itself was a relatively new network connecting all research and education personnel to both hospital databases and also to databases on the World Wide Web (WWW).
2. *Application.* The mission of the newly proposed BBS system was to link rural sites together, with the host acting as the "hub" of activity. Information, training, and education would radiate from the hub to rural areas as well as pass directly from remote site to remote site. Access to hospital and worldwide databases and libraries was viewed as secondary need; therefore, integrating these types of networked services would be Phase II of the project. Therefore, based on anticipated application, a stand-alone network seemed appropriate.

Remote-Site Analysis

Several informal group meetings with the administrators of the rural hospitals and clinics indicated that the facilities were all in difficult financial positions. Forced to work with limited resources, the rural administrators were looking for cost-effective alternatives for bringing health care services, information, education, and training to their communities.

The majority of the visits were challenging. The primary reason was the natural tendency of the rural hospital/clinic to question the motives of a large, profitable, urban hospital. This challenge was met head on with openness and honesty. Listening to the needs of the small clinic/hospital was key. Other challenges faced at initial remote site visits included the following:

1. *Overcoming the natural resistance to break from the past and to try something new.* Solution: Come prepared with an outline of scheduled or proposed training, education, communication events; bring representatives from service/training areas involved; bring a laptop to demonstrate applications; have someone at host site on-line to demonstrate synchronous communication options.

2. *Working within rigid budgets.* Solution: Make the venture as inexpensive as possible. Use existing computers, shareware communications software. Purchase modem only (a little more than $300). Some remote sites did not have $300 extra but were willing to find a way to raise the money—through bake sales and so on.

3. *The PBX (private branch exchange)-driven telephone network.* Because of network configuration, the computer/modem could not directly access an outside line. Solution: Reconfigure PBX to allow installation of a direct line to the computer. (Research of the local phone company found that the problem could be solved with approximately 2 hours of labor charges from telephone company @ $60.00/hr.)

4. *Old technology that exists in rural clinics.* Most sites had 486X computers. Solution: Design a flexible hybrid system that includes both old and new computer units. One possibility is to refurbish old PCs to the highest possible level and use them as server units to newer PCs.

5. *Old, noisy copper lines.* The excessive interference caused calls from some remote sites to abort erratically. Solution: Purchase a high-quality modem. Make sure the modem has V.32bis/ V.42/V.42bis capabilities and that the corresponding communications package provides ZMODEM transfer protocol.

🖉 $$ COST FACTORS $$

Development Time for a
Computer-Assisted Instruction Disk—CD-ROM

The following example describes the resources—both human and monetary—associated with designing, developing, and producing a computer-assisted instruction (CAI) resource disk to supplement a distance learning activity. Production in a four-phase process consisted of

- ❖ script writing
- ❖ storyboarding
- ❖ screen development
- ❖ formative evaluation (program rewrites)

Phase 1: Script Writing (3 hours)

This first phase in the process of producing a computerized training disk has three steps. In Step 1, the instructional designer meets with a team of content experts whose traditional materials are being converted to the computerized instructional medium. The purpose of the meeting is to introduce the team to the concept of computer-based training and to clearly outline what the instructional designer will need from the content experts to produce the materials. The primary focus of this meeting is to help the content experts see how their clean and complete input "up front" will save the designer and his or her production team time and therefore money in the development stages. The second key element of the process—storyboarding—is introduced and illustrated to the content experts at this time.

Phase 2: Storyboarding (50 hours)

This second phase of the project is time intensive for the instructional designer who will take the master outline developed by the team of content experts, along with all the materials that need to be incorporated into the development process (photographs, charts, video clips, etc.), and develop the exact order and linkages of computer screens that conceptually "do" what the content team has described. In the simplest of scenarios, provisions need to be made for both the students who (a) choose all the steps in order and progress to the end of the module and (b) those who do not and therefore need to be channeled back to the appropriate modules to review concepts missed. This process may sound simplistic, but it is actually quite involved and time intensive. As a rule of thumb, developers spend at least one-half hour per screen—charting, planning, and coding the sequences for the logical progression of computer screens to be developed. And it is not unusual for a complete tutorial to contain upward of 100 linked computer screens.

Phase 3: Screen Development (150 hours)

This third phase of the project involves the actual hands-on development of the program as outlined by the instructional designer. It is not unusual for each of the 100 screens described thus far to have as many as six "overlays" to create the proper linkages, as well as interest-grabbing effects (animation sequences, hypertext). The screen development process, then, would break down this way:

- ❖ 6 segments per screen
- ❖ 15 minutes per segment (work time)
- ❖ 5 segments × 15 minutes = 1.5 hours per screen
- ❖ 100 screens × 1.5 hours = 150 hours of production time

Phase 4: Formative Evaluation (Rewrites) (105 hours)

The fourth and final phase of the project requires that the product be evaluated and tested on many levels. Does it meet the expectations and goals of the instructor? Are the progressions, explanations, and sequences logical to the students? Has the information been put together in a way that enhances the learning process?

Observations and Conclusions

As you review the entire process presented, you find that a total of 325 hours may be required to create one 1-hour program segment. At first glance, this may seem as though the investment is not worth the time and effort. As you further consider the scope of the project, however, you realize that once the work is done . . . it is done. The same product can be used time after time, with little or no maintenance or updating. In addition, the final product can earn money back through outside sales. Therefore, in the long run, developing your own computer-based instructional disks can be a cost-effective practice.

Providing a Positive Distance Learning Experience

SCENARIO

You are the distance learning specialist for a telephone company just getting started in distance learning. You are in the process of preparing instructors for the distance learning environment.

YOUR TASK

Help your instructors design primary and secondary delivery media that will most appropriately "fit" the course objectives.

DISCUSSION . . .

CHAPTER 4

Speeding Up Technology Transfer

When teaching and training professionals are asked to participate in open and/or distance learning projects, many have an underlying resistance to change. Often, this resistance stems from internal perceptions and fears related to themselves, their students, and the technologies. Will they "lose face" with students/peers/subordinates while they are in the transitional process of mastering the technology and the environment? Do they have the ability to achieve competence and mastery of the elements? Will the technology and its problems control them? Will the extra time and effort expended be worth it: That is, will this project be here next year?

Chapter 4 takes a look at these very natural feelings and offers practical, step-by-step ideas to help teachers and trainers through this transitional change process.

Resisting Change Is a Natural Reaction

Resistance to change or resistance to trying something new is as normal and expected as night following day. Nowhere is this feeling of resistance greater than in situations in which instructors are finding it necessary to move to a technology-rich distance learning environment. From the body of research focused on open and distance learning, we know that the greatest barriers that instructors face have to do with establishing a "comfort zone"—feeling good about

- working with the new technology,
- adapting to changing teaching role, and
- helping students adapt to their changing role as distant learners.

Speeding up the actual transfer of technology—that is, learning to work through these issues quickly—can be broken into two main parts: (a) identifying what barriers to change already exist, in relation to either learning or the educational setting and (b) identifying what comfort zones exist for the learner(s) and the educator or trainer in relation to learning new things and trying new experiences.

Identifying the Barriers: Role of Perceptions

The importance of learner and educator/trainer perspective to how quickly and how much change occurs has been well documented for many years. This portion of our reality plays an important role in how we adapt to change. The philosopher Karl R. Popper (1972) sees our reality as really three worlds interacting to varying degrees: The first is the physical world around us that we can see, touch, or smell. The second part is the individual's own life experiences, which extend beyond the physical to include subjective elements. The third part consists of the huge amount of data, information, and knowledge that these life experiences bring. Often labeled *objective* because humans use procedures or standards to collect and analyze it, this third part continues its existence independently of our subjective life experiences. This feedback loop of our past life experience interacts less with the other two parts, but it is in the background, constantly acting on us, causing us to react in return. Another way of referring to this third world or part is our "symbolic environment" (Paprock, 1993), which everyone must adapt to. Scientists who study human beings repeatedly emphasize this: To a large extent, humans adapt through learning. To function normally, a person must assimilate a considerable proportion of the contents of that third world or part. Because the process is ongoing, constant selectivity is required.

Human learning capacity provides us with a basis for ongoing, almost limitless, adaptation to the environment. However, our emotional, psychological, and social needs constrain the adaptive range within which our learning ability can operate. This is what leads to problems in adjustment such as Toffler's (1971) "future shock,"—the failure to adapt when too many changes occur around us and the rate of change in our environment is exceedingly rapid (p. 26). For most adults, the typical monthly round of activities and thoughts tends to reinforce stability and minimize change. Major influences that encourage stability include societal values, role expectations, personality, interests, activities, habits, and interactions (Knox, 1986). These same influences may act to encourage change.

It is typically easier or more comfortable to think and do things the same way unless boredom, frustration, or external circumstances precipitate a change (Brookfield, 1984; Paprock, 1993).

As we talk about speeding up the actual transfer of technology, we begin to realize that the starting point for rapid and successful change usually comes from somewhere inside the individual's comfort zone.

There is no denying that change can be rapid and successful in a crisis situation that is both uncomfortable and unfamiliar to the individual, but these extreme events occur less frequently in relation to distance learning than in natural disasters. Changes introduced to individuals who are somewhat comfortable shorten the time needed for the introduction and increase the amount of learning that occurs. Carl Rogers is often cited for his belief that one needs to provide a safe place for learners to explore themselves and their environments. Rogers (1961) also emphasized that our natural tendency as learners is to confine ourselves to those domains in which we already feel safe or comfortable. To achieve success, we need to help learners reach the limits of their safe or comfortable domains and move on into those fear-producing or uncomfortable domains. The rewards will be having individuals become active seekers after new developments.

Identifying the Barriers: Reactions to Fear

> *Two important components of overcoming fear and successfully handling change are (a) assuming a sense of openness and (b) consciously taking control over that openness.*

Fear of the unknown is a barrier to change. Learners and educators or trainers respond to fear in four basic ways: They may shut it out, denying the existence of anything new or that contradicts previous experience. These are people who are so busy pretending that all is as it has been that they can no longer deal with reality—for example, educators or trainers who type out and manually grades their own tests to be sure no one can steal the questions or answers instead of using a computer program with an automated question library, test generator, grade book, and test analyzer. Another example is the exhausted educator or trainer who refuses to acknowledge either his or her waning physical condition or newer technologies and instead travels hundreds of miles each day or week to teach a class in person instead of converting it to a distance learning class.

The second type of response to fear is to open up all the way to it, seeking new experiences constantly. People can carry this approach to extremes that leave them totally unable to cope. One example would be instructors or trainers who are always getting and using the newest, even untested, technology or programs in their classes. They do not control or feel in control of their actions. The technology and its problems control the person. Falling short of this extreme response to fear is the third type of response.

The third response is when a minimum return of equilibrium is achieved by substituting one behavior that is a little less fearful for another that held the initial fear. But the fear factor is not eliminated and at another time or place may have to be faced again. An example might be students who transfer out of classes that require writing assignments done on computers because they fear using computers. They reduce their fear this time, but because computers are a part of their chosen job, the fear will have to be faced again.

The fourth and best possible response to the fear is for people to grow and develop. They are able to do this by incorporating the new experiences and information in such a way that they are changed. The two important features of this successful change are their openness and their perceived control over that openness.

Identifying the Comfort Zone: Reducing or Preventing Barriers to Technology Transfer

Success working with the new technology builds the foundation for future successes.

In any new or "unknown" situation, it is always easiest to start from where you are developmentally—to use what you know to get you through. We refer to this natural tendency to build on what you already know to help you around the barriers of a new experience as "piggybacking." You can speed up the technology transfer process by piggybacking different distance learning technologies in such a way that at least one is familiar in a comfortable way and does not cause fear for the instructor/trainer or learner fear; both openness and a sense of control are maintained. What this process allows is a transfer of prior coping skills to the new situation. Success in this new situation with the new technology builds a foundation for future successes while changing the person into an active seeker of new distance learning technologies.

Remember that open and distance learning are rooted in correspondence study and built on the same piggybacking techniques we've been talking about. As new technologies were introduced and people became comfortable using them, the natural tendency was to enhance and enrich the distance learning environment by incorporating the new technologies. In this way, several distinct levels of distance learning activities evolved through the years.

The Problem With Getting Too Comfortable

The role of discomfort is a central theme for learning to occur. That theme is particularly relevant to distance education, where many teachers and learners experience discomfort. For learners to attain optimal states of growth, they need to enter discomfort-producing conditions (Joyce, 1983; Van Doren, 1977). Significant growth requires the learner to manage discomfort productively. If a person is too comfortable with what's known, there is no reason to go to the unknown.

Thelen (1960) states, "The learner does not learn unless he [or she] does not know how to respond." He claims that group investigation begins with "a stimulus situation to which students . . . can react and discover basic conflicts among their attitudes, ideas, and modes of perception" (p. 81).

Interpreters of Carl Rogers frequently concentrate on his argument for providing a safe place for learners to explore themselves and their environments. Rogers (1961) also emphasizes that our natural tendency as learners is to confine ourselves to those domains in which we already feel safe. A major task is to help learners reach into those domains shrouded in fear—to help us become active seekers after new development.

Hunt (1971) stresses the relationship of environment to development. If the environment is too comfortable or "reliable," the learners will be satisfied at the stage of concrete thinking where the ability to integrate new information and form new conceptual schemes is limited. Although approaching development in a very different way from Thelen, Hunt states explicitly that discomfort is a precursor to growth.

Too much mismatch or discomfort can be overwhelming. The idea is to create a situation in which persons are uncomfortable in a comfortable situation: That is, learners should not be afraid to take risks. In the arena of distance education, instructors can use the discomfort caused by a new learning environment to benefit both their own development and that of their students.

Overcoming Resistance

On the following pages are case studies describing how others have overcome resistance to change by building on the comfortable and familiar.

✐ CASE STUDY INTRODUCTORY INFORMATION

About the project:

When a local hospital wanted to start teaching its continuing education classes as distance education classes, its nursing instructors expressed fears that (a) the programs would not be effective and (b) they would not know how to use the new technology. To increase the comfort level of the instructors, the decision was made to create a multimodel distance learning format that allowed for the inclusion of "familiar" teaching techniques and media with the "new" teaching techniques and technologies.

About the participants:

These were nurses who worked on 24-hour wards and critical care units in two separate buildings physically separated by two miles—that is, "at a distance." Although scheduled on 12-hour shifts, the nurses were also required to attend mandatory continuing education classes to maintain their licenses. The traditional classes were offered during the day, Monday through Friday, in an administration and education building separate from the two patient care buildings. Distance learning opportunities were seen as a way to make the mandatory education more accessible. Most of the nurses had never participated in distance learning classes before this time.

CASE STUDY 1

Level 1 Technology Transfer Process: Passive to Moderate Interaction

In this example, five face-to-face classes were refitted for distance learning delivery via computer tutorials (computer-assisted instruction [CAI] and computer simulations). Multimedia workstations were set up at the distant sites to implement the teaching/training. CAI was the primary means of instructional delivery. Supporting media included printed materials, audio-conferencing, electronic bulletin boards (e-mail), Internet, and World Wide Web communications, and research activities.

Background

- The programmer carefully followed the book outline while developing the lesson screens.
- The CAIs and tutorials were (a) preloaded on workstations and (b) available for distribution in disk format for those students who had personal computers (PCs) at home.
- Participants were given access to the local area network's BBS, including the Internet and the World Wide Web.
- All instructions, agendas, assignments, and so on were located "on-line."
- Step-by-step instructions were also available in print form.
- The modules were constructed in a hypermedia environment. In this setting, students could "browse" the lessons, choosing which "series" they would do at a sitting. Each series of modules represented specific learning objectives that the instructor wanted them to cover. Once a series of modules was chosen, students were committed to completing all modules before going on to a new topic. Letting students access learning in whatever order seemed logical to them allowed for individuality and for differences in learning styles.
- Each lesson provided current feedback to nurses on the number of lessons they had completed and the number of questions they answered correctly.
- Each lesson also had built-in pretests and posttests for immediate feedback and understanding.
- Feedback was given for both correct and incorrect answers. When students chose the correct answer, the computer screen "linked to" the next step in the process. When students chose the incorrect answer, the

computer screen linked to a series of reinforcement "stacks" that filled in for students the information they were missing.
- On completion of the program, students' scores were sent to the education office, and a certificate of completion was sent out to the nurse.
- The screens that made up the computer-based instruction tutorials could also be printed as hard copies for study purposes.

This example is given as passive to moderately interactive because the majority of the learning that occurred was from student interaction with materials rather than with instructor or peers.

✎ CASE STUDY 2

Level 2 Technology Transfer Process: Moderate Interaction

In this example, classes were refitted for distance learning delivery by using existing technologies in new ways. Technologies included speaker telephones, fax machines, CAI software, PCs that were upgraded to multimedia workstations and loaded with BBS/Internet/World Wide Web software, and printed materials. The BBS was the primary means of instructional delivery; supporting media included printed materials, fax materials, audioconferencing, and CAI tutorials.

Background

- The nursing department had telephones with speakers, fax machines, PCs with local area network (LAN) communication capabilities, and an automated CAI program for learning to manage patient registration. Until this time, these resources were used separately; they were not used together for a teaching application.
- By using the methods described, faculty members were able to move from a Level 1 experience—very passive and disconnected, as in the previous example—to a Level 2 distance learning experience. This was accomplished by integrating the telecommunications technologies into the class design, creating a moderately interactive multimodel distance learning environment.
- Students/nurses were required to attend a series of preclass training sessions where they learned to log onto and navigate through the BBS. The emphasis of the training was not only for sending and receiving e-mail but also for participating in live interactive "conferences" (computer-mediated conferencing). Eight hours of training were required, although the computer lab technicians were available 5 days a week.
- The primary form of instruction was the BBS. Students met on-line at a specific time twice each week.
- Speaker phones, faxes, and cameras attached to the PCs with special videoconferencing software were set up to enhance the learning environment and to allow for impromptu questions, clarifications, and explanations.
- CAI was required to be completed individually between classes.
- At the end of the 60-day test period, the rate of nursing staff members successfully completing the required lessons increased to 98% after the implementation of the multimodel distance learning experience. In the

previous year, the nursing department had averaged 80% to 85% compliance by the nurses attending the required continuing education classes.

This example is given as moderately interactive because even though BBS was the primary means of delivery, the learning that occurred was primarily from student interaction with the instructor and with peers. Interaction with supporting media was supplemental.

Elements of Success

These programs were successful because the nursing educators who were a part of the new multimodel distance learning project were encouraged to "start from what they knew"—from what was familiar and comfortable. These nursing faculty members had a positive first distance learning experience and were able to decrease barriers to staff members' learning and using the new distance learning technologies. Following are some of the reasons these instructors experienced a smooth transition into multimodel distance learning. They moved from known to unknown by

- conducting a thorough program needs assessments—just as they would for any solid face-to-face teaching experience,
- engaging in a series of short, formative student evaluations, and
- using the primary base of technology they were already comfortable with (fax, speaker phones, written materials)

Using this approach, faculty members were able to overcome the top seven barriers to traditional and/or distance learning teaching experiences:

- Faulty knowledge and weak skills their staff already possessed
- Negative feelings that staff members held about their ability to learn (lack of self-confidence for learning)
- Lack of staff member comfort about learning with others around
- Lack of interest in or energy to learning
- Social or family needs that affect the learning requirements
  ❖ Location and time conflicts
  ❖ Quality issues related to the knowledge and teaching skills of instructors

The biggest benefit from this technology transfer (change) process was that nursing staff members learned from firsthand experience how they can successfully adapt and adjust their attitudes toward distance learning technologies. The piggyback approach for introducing the new distance learning technologies allowed learners to draw on familiar images and procedures to decrease the transfer time as they problem solved their way through the CAIs and or the written self-paced learning booklets.

A Few Observations About Change

A close look at teaching and training professionals who are asked to participate in open and/or distance learning projects reveals that many have an underlying resistance to change. However, from our years of combined experience with open and distance teaching, we have found that in professionals who are self-confident, open, and willing to move beyond their "comfort zones," fear is good! Their very real apprehensions and fears give rise to traits that can actually act as catalysts for positive transformation. One trait is the proclivity to value the instincts caused by their fears, intuitively treating what others see as "stumbling blocks" as opportunities for positive discovery. This trait makes them ideal student and presenter advocates for open and distance learning environments, because every aspect of the experience is positively enhanced. For example, take the stumbling block of program development; problems can be detected earlier, speeding up the sequential planning and production processes.

A second trait of these professionals is the need to continually question why items are needed. This trait is valuable throughout the refining and assimilation processes to come. This process of continually questioning, identifying, and verbalizing reactions and instincts helps form the much-needed boundaries in which the focus is on the learner and the goal of learning, not on the technology alone.

Fears, when recognized and made manageable by self-confident professionals, open and willing to move beyond their comfort zones, create a stronger team member for the open and distance learning/teaching environment.

In the two case studies you've just read, the primary methods of delivery for the distance learning environment were computer-aided instruction and computer-mediated conferencing and learning. In these examples, most of the task of helping learners get comfortable with their environment was thought through and organized "behind the scenes" by the distance learning instructor. But there are also many things you can do to help make the transitional process easier. On the following pages, we discuss ways to help you make the transition to yet another distance learning setting—the two-way interactive video environment.

Optimizing Familiar Applications

Adapting Workspace and Room Setups

 THE QUESTION:

If this new environment is going to work for me, I need to be comfortable. How do I speed up the process?

THE ANSWER:

All too often, technology-rich distance education environments, like the sorcerer's apprentice, tend to take over the activities and become their own justification. Students as well as instructors can easily fall into the enchantment of being controlled by the technology rather than controlling it. Your experience teaching from a distance will be more gratifying if you begin by identifying the actual classroom behaviors that make up your teaching style and merge these behaviors into the whole of your specific distance learning environment rather than letting the "technology rule."

Think about how you are most comfortable teaching. Do you stand at a podium? Walk around the room? Sit with students? These preferences and characteristics that you carry from classroom to classroom are a part of your teaching style.

The technology should enhance your teaching style, not hinder it. This is what we refer to as optimizing instructor workspace.

 THE QUESTION:

How do I get started?

☞ THE ANSWER:

Optimizing your workspace:
You can optimize your workspace by making choices that compliment your teaching style. For example, begin with the way you are most comfortable teaching. When you teach, you probably prefer to

- sit,
- stand, or
- pace.

Your equipment choices and setup should reflect your preference. For example:

If your natural tendency is to sit while you teach, arrange your workspace so that all of the equipment you will use is within easy reaching distance.

This will help . . .

☐ Set up equipment and seating area somewhere within the student workspace to help shift the focus away from you and onto the students.

☐ Give yourself plenty of workspace.

☐ Place "tape marks" on the floor to mark chair position.

☐ Preset a variety of camera shots: one close head shot for emphasis; one pulled back a few feet for variety.

> ☐ Be aware that even though most cameras are automatic focus, they have depth range of approximately 3 feet. Therefore, position your chair in the middle of that 3-foot field of vision. That is, position chair so as to allow about 1.5 feet for the times you will comfortably "lean into" the camera for emphasis and 1.5 feet for the times you will "lean back" to give a visual and mental break to students.

If your natural tendency is to stand at a podium while you teach, you will have limited workspace. Check around. Many vendors offer a compact teaching podium or workstation equipped with basic equipment built in and with fold-out extensions to place your materials. Still, you may find that setting up additional workspace is highly desirable.

> **This will help . . .**
>
> ☐ Teaching from a podium can be limiting. Always be aware of what the learners are seeing!
> ☐ Try to add variety wherever you can; if you are teaching a televideo class, set a variety of camera shots: one close head shot for emphasis; one pulled back a few feet for more variety.

If your natural tendency is to pace or wander . . . you're in luck! In the current climate of rapidly evolving technologies, most vendors have refined and enhanced compression algorithms, cameras, and instructor and student mics to the point that movement is hardly a problem. Handling your pacing tendency, then, will be a matter of taking time to understand the capabilities of your equipment and blocking off time each week to practice. The more you practice the more comfortable, competent, and confident (C^3) you become and the less the technology gets in the way of your natural teaching flow.

> **This will help...**
>
> ☐ In both computer- and video-based classes, use a facilitator or ask a student or colleague to assist you during your first classes. This person can make camera changes, cue up slides, computer graphics, and so on.
>
> ☐ In both video- and computer-based teletraining, set off a "pacing" area with tape markings on floor to keep you in viewing and audio range.
>
> ☐ Place a stool at one end of pacing area for sitting.
>
> ☐ Select an area with an uncluttered background (clutter can cause screen to flicker at remote end).
>
> ☐ For televideo classes, in the next buying cycle, budget in a "tracking camera."
>
> **In PC-based teletraining, choose someone with prior experience to operate the computer that is televised in the front of the room.**

Figure 4.1 shows an example of a room set up for all three worlds.

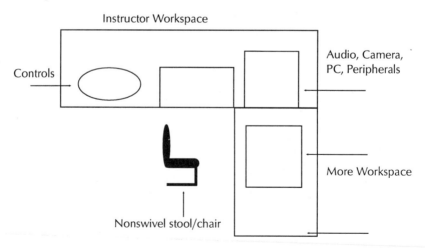

Figure 4.1. Room Set Up for All Three Worlds

THE QUESTION:

How can I make my students comfortable?

☞ THE ANSWER:

By doing the same kinds of things you did to make yourself comfortable . . . optimizing students' workspace.

At both local and remote sites, it will be important that all learners can

- hear and be heard,
- see and be seen.

You will find that in every class, there will be those learners who are "camera shy" and try to avoid being seen and heard. It's important that you recognize and deal with this scenario up front and plan camera and desk/table placement so that the problem does not get out of hand, disrupting the flow of energy and activity for the rest of the class.

☆ By optimizing both instructor and learner workspace from the start, you will encourage the following things to happen:

- ☆ Create a highly focused learning atmosphere
- ☆ Shift center of focus from instructor to learner
- ☆ Encourage and create peer to peer collaboration
- ☆ Increase student/teacher interaction
- ☆ Increase student/materials interaction
- ☆ Create healthy competition, camaraderie, and teamwork among multiple sites

The result . . . a highly charged, highly interactive teaching/learning environment.

Some Teleteaching Basics

The following section gives a general overview that will help you begin to work with the basic equipment of the teleteaching environment. The primary areas of consideration are these:

- Video and audio basics
- Working with equipment
- Optimizing familiar educational applications

Speeding Up Technology Transfer 93

Table 4.1 shows a checklist of basics that apply to audio, PC-based, video, and multimodel distance learning applications.

TABLE 4.1 Audio and Video Basics

Audio Basics

- Don't Shout!
    Mics can pick up sounds 18" to 3' or more away.
    Speak clearly, with good voice projection.
    Speak naturally.
- Speak one at a time.
- Keep comments short.
- Be conscious of phrasing, pacing of speech.
- Remember—sound is directional and is therefore affected by quick, frequent head movements.

Working With Mics

- Try not to mute mics for long periods of time.
    Distant class loses sense of community
    Distant class becomes distracted
    With mute in effect, local class also suffers
    Loses spontaneous comments
    Lulls class into passiveness
    Causes additional delays in audio response time
- Face toward participants, away from audio speakers to avoid feedback.
- Audio feedback or clipping? Turn volume down at REMOTE site by pressing the DOWN arrow in audio control area of control table or handheld remote control.
- Still can't hear? Make sure everyone is in range of mics and that mics are not covered by books, papers, and the like.

Video Basics

- Adjust cameras to display important visual elements.
- Preset multiple camera for (a) variety and (b) easy access to key instructional elements.
- Be aware of what camera you are sending! Switching to another camera? A white board? Remember what you are "sending."
- Be conscious of "personal space": Don't set cameras so close to student's face they are uncomfortable.
- Set cameras to allow all students to be viewed when speaking.

The following reference guide is a tool you can use before and during the teleclass.

Quick Reference Guide: Working With the Equipment

Key names and telephone numbers:
    Site coordinator_____
    System phone _____
    System fax _____
    Help line _____
    Audio bridge _____
    Remote site(s) _____
    Others _____
    Others _____

Quick Start:
- ☐ Turn system on
- ☐ Where is system on switch? _____
- ☐ Turn mics/monitors on
- ☐ Where are mic/monitor on switches? _____
- ☐ Check physical equipment connections
- ☐ Turn on user interface(s) (remote control, graphics tablet, touch screen, power pack)
- ☐ Where are user interface buttons/switches? _____
- ☐ Check connection with remote sites
- ☐ Arrange room layout
- ☐ Organize teaching space/work area

Quick Start:
Test instructor AND student computers/cameras to see that connections are working.

Most classes will have multiple systems. Each computer/camera/workstation will have a different name or number. So that you do not get confused during the class, record those numbers here:

Computer/camera 1 _____
Computer/camera 2 _____
Computer/camera 3 _____
And so on . . .

Using peripherals? (CD-ROM, See Me/See You Cameras, etc.) Most systems have outputs for two to four additional video outputs for peripheral video equipment, such as a VCR. List those connections here:

Peripheral 1:   Name _____
              Connection location _____
Peripheral 2:   Name _____
              Connection location _____
Peripheral 3:   Name _____
              Connection location _____

Additional Peripheral Audio Checklist

Infrared "Follow Me" Mics
- ☐ Place "necklace" on, making sure front and back "beads" are not covered by hair or clothing.
- ☐ Turn power on.
- ☐ Set volume.
- ☐ Select "home" to activate camera tracking.
- ☐ Preset multiple shots: close for still; far for pacing.

> Hints
>
> Remember to take off during breaks!
>
> If you are 5'4" or shorter, you may want to use a safety pin to pin the necklace of the tracking camera so that the tracking bead is closer to your face. This is because the way the camera tracks is to find the bead and then focus on an area equally above and below it. If the bead is sitting too low on your body, the camera can focus on an unbecoming shot of you—that is, from your neck down!

Lavaliere Mics
- ☐ Clip on mic.
- ☐ Turn power on.
- ☐ Set volume.
- ☐ Note: Remember to take off during breaks!

Student (Table) Microphones
- ☐ Turn mics on.
- ☐ Uncover mics.
- ☐ Face mics toward participants, away from audio speakers (to avoid feedback).
- ☐ Mics can pick up sounds 18" to 3' away.

Familiar Educational Applications in Open and Distance Learning Environments

Once you begin to get comfortable teaching from a distance, you will realize that every media accessory you ever used is "rolled" into the media conferencing system. Most instructors say that when they taught in a traditional environment, they had to choose which *one* media they would use. In a distance learning environment, not one but *all* media are typically available to use at the same time. The convenience and variety please most instructors.

The following section

- highlights most commonly used media,
- demonstrates the most effective multimodel designs, and
- lists pros and cons of each choice.

The VCR (Videocassette Recorder)

How is the VCR used as a teaching tool?

- To play a tape for viewing
- To record site participants (local or remote)
- To record instruction for library backup and review
- As a teaching strategy, use VCR recordings to

   present demonstration material,
   present opportunity for interactive questions and answers,
   add humor, and
   provide students with a "listening break."

In both computer-based and interactive video applications, you can capture still "snapshots" of key segments of the film to be retrieved for later use. Here's an example from a videoconferencing application: A sociology professor we know uses video snapshots from the film *Sister Act* to illustrate the effect that environment has on behavior. She viewed the film before class on the VCR attached to the videoconferencing system and captured and stored segments as still graphics. During the class, the students were told to look for visual cues in the movie that the environment was having an effect on the main character. During the discussion that followed viewing the movie, the instructor presented each of the graphics she had captured and stored, illustrating the changes in behavior being discussed. The end result: Still graphics captured from video provided a powerful teaching tool for aiding memory and retention.

☆ Helpful Hints

- ☆ Limit video segment to 5 to 7 minutes.
- ☆ Prepare activities to accompany showing of tape (i.e., looking for answers to prepared questions).
- ☆ Send a copy of video to all sites (in case of transmission problems, the remote sites will have the material they need to continue class).

Live (3-Dimensional) Objects

How are live (3-dimensional) objects used as a teaching tool?

- To simulate real-life tasks or equipment
- To demonstrate processes or procedures
- To depict conceptual models

☆ Helpful Hints

☆ To increase effectiveness, send duplicate objects to each site.

☆ "Chunk" your presentation into 7- to 15-minute segments that (a) teach application, (b) provide time for hands-on practice, and (c) provide time to relate experience to own life work.

☆ Whenever possible, build learner confidence through "learning by doing."

☆ Arrange for remote site facilitator/preceptor whenever possible.

☆ Use true-to-life size/scale objects for easiest transfer of learning.

Overheads, Transparencies, and 35 mm Slides

How are overheads, transparencies, and 35 mm slides used as teaching tools?

The same as they were used in a traditional class!

- To reinforce written, verbal information with a visual depiction
- To integrate photographs, charts, and graphs into the lesson (especially good for high-intensity graphics; camera picks up fine detailing, definition)
- To bring in time-line dimensions (e.g., movement of clouds over a 4-hour period; historic time continuums)
- To decrease bias or instructor influence by allowing students to make their own interpretations

☆ Helpful Hints

- ☆ Depending on lighting, clear transparencies may "glare." A better solution is to create transparencies with dark backgrounds (blue, black, purple, green, brown) and light text (yellow, white, cream, blue). However, if you have a bottom light panel, clear transparencies with black text will work okay.
- ☆ You'll get best results with 35 mm slides created in a 3 × 4 landscape format with large, readable lettering (for every 6 feet of distance from the viewing screen, add ¼ inch to the font size).
- ☆ Place your 35 mm slides/transparencies in clear plastic sleeves for transport and display. The ones we're referring to can fit in a 3-ring note binder that holds up to 24 slides. The advantage is that your slides stay organized, transport easier, and can be displayed right from the plastic sleeve.

Digitized Computer Graphics

So far, we have been trying to illustrate that you can easily incorporate existing materials into the two-way interactive teleteaching environment. Digitized computer graphics, however, offer by far the most flexibility to teleteachers. If you are using computer graphics, following are some of the advantages you will notice. If you are not, here are some reasons you may want to begin using digitized graphics:

How are digitized computer graphics used as a teaching tool?

- Serve as framework to "hang" presentation
- Increase instructor comfort and confidence level
- Are more legible, concise, easier to read; therefore build learners' confidence and satisfaction
- Transferred to hard copy as part of student workbooks, digital graphics enhance learning
- Help organize instructor: Structure flow of activities
- Create a more productive use of class time
- Enable complex details to be easily displayed
- Can double as class notes and study guides
- Are easily modified, updated
- Are convenient and cut down instructor work time . . . once they're done, they're done

☆ Helpful Hints

- ☆ Limit graphics to 20 per 50-minute segment.
- ☆ Limit graphic on-screen time to 15 seconds.
- ☆ Use fonts no smaller than 28 point (appx. 1/4 inch per every 6 feet from screen).
- ☆ Show key points only! (as opposed to complete paragraphs of text).

☆ Remember, primary purpose of computer graphics is enhanced readability.
  - Provide reinforcement for retention
  - Help distant learners maintain attention
  - Build distant learners' confidence, understanding
  - Serve as "advanced organizer" so everyone is "on the same page"

☆ Send hard copies of all graphics to remote sites as "backup":
  - In case of technical problems
  - For references to accompany lesson
  - For library of materials, available to absent students

Table 4.2 will give you an idea of how easily some commonly used teaching materials and media can/cannot be integrated into a multi-model distance learning design.

TABLE 4.2 Media and Materials

	Audio	Video	PC-Based	Multimodel
Videocassette recorder (VCR)	—	X	X	X
Live (3-dimensional) objects	—	X	X	X
Overhead transparencies	—	X	—	X
35 mm slides	—	X	X	X
Handmade graphics	—	X	X	X
External devices:				
Flip charts	—	X	X	X
Whiteboards	—	X	X	X
Chalkboards	—	—	—	—

Assimilating Your Teaching Methods to Fit a Multimodel Design

SCENARIO

You are the local teacher of mathematics/business studies. Your primary method of teaching is through presentation of case studies and case problems.

YOUR TASK

Figure out how YOU CAN COMFORTABLY assimilate the case studies/case problems techniques you are familiar with into a multimodel design (mix-and-match technologies).

DISCUSSION . . .

CHAPTER 5

Designing Instruction for Learning

One of the biggest fears of first-time teleteaching instructors is the belief that teaching from a distance is radically different from teaching face-to-face. Although it is true that there are differences, it is also true that the basic principles for teaching and learning from a distance are the same as the basic principles for any teaching and learning environment. Instructors still need to address issues such as program purpose and the volume of information that students must learn, but managing these areas calls for a difference of emphasis in a technology-based learning environment.

In Chapter 5, we will look at ways to help you refocus your emphasis:

1. Organizing your time and instruction
2. Becoming aware of your presentation style and personal image
3. Developing participative teaching methods and techniques

What's the Same?

 THE QUESTION:

When it comes to teaching, is there *anything* I can do the way I did before? What things are the same?

 THE ANSWER:

The answer—as you will recall from earlier discussions—is that you can do quite a bit the same: You can continue to design and develop good, solid instructional design models for your teaching. No matter what the teaching/training situation, the bottom line is this:

- Good instructional design produces good outcomes, and poor instructional design produces poor outcomes.
- Learning does not take place because of what the teacher does but because of what the learner does.
- The measure of good instructional design is the meaningfulness of the learning that takes place.

Meaningful Learning

 THE QUESTION:

What is meaningful learning?

 THE ANSWER:

Meaningful learning is defined as *learning in which individuals are helped to acquire needed knowledge, attitudes, and skills to help solve real life problems.* When one works with adult learners, it becomes clear that the desire of most adult learners is for teachers to make information meaningful. From the research of adult education, we know that meaningful learning occurs when learners are drawn into the learning activity.

Designing Instruction for Learning   107

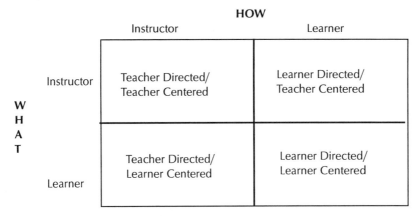

Figure 5.1. Models of Teaching

The terms *involvement, participation,* and *interaction* are often used interchangeably to describe this process.

Models of Teaching

No matter which term is used, the point is that an important relationship does exist between meaningful learning and the extent to which learners are involved in "what" is taught and "how" it is taught. The more involved the learner is in defining the learning equation, the more interaction and participation will occur (Paprock & Williams, 1993). This insight led Paprock and Williams (1993) to develop a 2 × 2 matrix illustrating the concept (see Figure 5.1).

Figure 5.1 suggests that in any teaching/learning process, there are two sets of considerations: *what* is learned and *how* it is learned. The decisions made about the relationship between these two elements of an instructional design model affect extent of participation and interaction.

Extent of Participation

 THE QUESTION:

What do you mean by the extent of participation?

108   DISTANCE LEARNING

☞ THE ANSWER:

The extent of participation refers to the many levels of interaction—mental, physical, and emotional—that keep learners involved in the learning process:

- Talking
- Writing
- "Watching for"
- Thinking
- Doing

In high-technology distance education environments, the key to creating highly interactive and participative learning environments is not getting so wrapped up in the technology that *the technology drives the method.* As in any learning environment, the basics of good instructional design remain the same:

- Participation and interaction enhance learning.
- The extent of participation is dictated by the content.
- The content determines the learning objectives.
- The objectives determine the teaching methods and techniques.
- Most important, the attributes of the learners determine the appropriateness of the above choices.

Relating back to ARCS model (see Chapter 1), the extent of participation and interaction are directly related to the learners' level of Attention, Relevance, Confidence, and Satisfaction, and these, in turn, are directly related to meaningful learning.

✋ THE QUESTION:

How do I use what I know about the nature of participation to create a distance education environment that encourages meaningful learning?

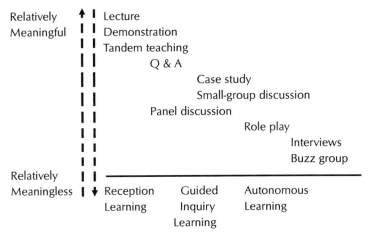

Figure 5.2. Methods of Teaching and Modes of Learning

☞ THE ANSWER:

As we begin to talk about meaningful learning in distance education, it is useful to use Ausubel's "modes of learning" (Ausubel, Novak, & Hanesian, 1978). Ausubel views learning as being in three forms: reception learning, guided inquiry, and autonomous learning. All three forms of learning can range from meaningful to meaningless.

Modes of Learning

In Figure 5.2, we have combined the various methods of teaching (lecture, group discussion, etc.) with Ausubel's modes of learning. The positioning of each method is more or less related to the nature of the resulting participation and interaction. For example, the traditional lecture falls into the area of "reception learning," whereas the small-group discussion falls between the areas of "guided inquiry" and "autonomous" learning.

Within Ausubel's framework, any method can range from meaningful to meaningless. No one method is "better" than another in creating meaningful learning. The meaningfulness of the learning that occurs depends on learner attributes—that is, where the learner is in his or her individual learning curve. When a meaningful learning set is present,

TABLE 5.1 What Is the Same

| | Instructional Design Strategies | | | |
Item Variable	Audio	Video	Computer	Multimodel
Activity level (passive to active)	Passive to moderately interactive	Passive to highly interactive	Moderately to highly interactive	Moderately to highly interactive
Preparation agenda	X	X	X	X
Good design = good outcome	X	X	X	X
Bad design = bad outcome	X	X	X	X
Bottom line = meaningful learning	X	X	X	X

Bottom Line: Learning takes place because of what the learner does.

| | Extent of Participation | | | |
Item Variable	Audio	Video	Computer	Multimodel
Talking	XX	X	LS	XX
Writing	X	X	LS	X
Watching/ listening for	X	X	XX	XX
Thinking	X	X	LS	X
Doing	LS	LS	LS	X

NOTE: Under each column heading, we have placed an X if the concept discussed requires a different emphasis in that delivery system as it is in a traditional teaching/training environment. Some entries have a XX (double X), which means that the differences are multifaceted and therefore require a different emphasis for their various parts. LS stands for "level specific," indicating that depending on the specific distance learning delivery tool, the characteristics might or might not be the same as in a traditional learning environment.

levels of interaction and participation increase. These can occur in any of a number of modes or methods of teaching. The "job" of the instructor is to find a fit between learner attributes, task, and content within the context of the attributes of the instructor and the technology.

We began this section by asking the question "What can we expect to be the same?" in a distance learning environment. A summary of the preceding discussion is given Table 5.1. What we've done is list for you the various distance learning delivery methods that you may be involved with. Under each column heading, we have placed an "X" if the concept discussed is the same in that delivery system as it is in a traditional teaching/training environment.

As you go through the following pages, keep in mind that our perspective is based on what we know from our experiences and from what the body of knowledge of open and distance learning tells us about the experiences of other distance educators and distance learners. As you begin to teach from a distance, you too will come to find that there are indeed differences, and they might or might not be significant, depending on your own personal situation.

What's Different?

 THE QUESTION:

What's different in open and distance learning environments?

☞ THE ANSWER:

It's been our experience that it's more a matter of a difference in emphasis in how you approach teaching than in how you construct your basic teaching design. You already *know* that the courses you've designed and teach are effective and successful. The challenge now is to reengineer those courses for distance learning, taking full advantage of the features of the technologies you now have available to you. We have found that the simplest way to get started in this process is to start with the way you

- prepare yourself,
- prepare your students, and
- prepare your materials.

"LESSONS LEARNED" FROM FIRST-TIME TELETEACHERS:

Insights and Understandings From First-Time Teleteachers

"It's important to let students know what they can expect to happen, and how they can be a part of the success of the class."

"I've had to get MUCH more organized and do more planning in terms of both instruction and materials . . . but it's made my face-to-face classes better too."

"Agendas and advanced organizers are important because they keep everyone on track, cue students on what they can expect, as well as what will be expected of them."

"I'm a traditional lecturer. I've found that I can keep on lecturing if I do it in shortened segments of about 15 minutes. If I punctuate my lecture with 'listening' and 'activity' breaks, I can keep on lecturing and distance learners don't get bored or lost."

Get comfortable with the environment: Plan, Prepare, Practice

Plan participative, learner-centered instruction

Prepare yourself: What to expect/what not to expect

Practice, practice, practice

Instruct and prepare students: What to expect/what *not* to expect

Begin to humanize (personalize) the teleclass even before the class begins!

Establish participation and feedback habits EARLY!

Keep students involved!

Talking

Writing

"Watching for"

Hands-on

Doing

Thinking

Designing Instruction for Learning 113

Prepare Yourself

Teaching in a live, interactive open or distance learning environment is different from teaching a class face-to-face. The most obvious differences are that the instructor is (a) separated by time and distance from some or all of the students; (b) working within a newly imposed, tight set of time constraints; and (c) teaching through a televised video format. You can make the most of these differences by paying close attention to these areas of preparation:

- Organizing your time
- Organizing your instruction
- Presentation style and personal image
- Participative teaching methods and techniques

Organize Your Time

Teaching in an open and/or distance learning environment requires an investment of your time: time to acclimate yourself to the technology and altered learning space and time to plan and prepare for the macro and micro details shown in Box 5.1.

Organize Your Instruction

Classes taught from a distance often have an exact start and end time, predetermined by network availability. If you need just a few more minutes to finish discussing an important point, you may not be able to extend the class as you would in a traditional classroom. Therefore, organizing your instruction takes on greater importance. Box 5.2 lists ways to organize your instruction.

Chart Your Presentation

Charting your presentation in advance will help you see the following:

- The type, scope, extent of advanced prep time needed
- If you have planned too much or too little
- What you need to do/show/chart/plan to get the results you want

BOX 5.1. Planning and Preparing for Details

Macro Level

- Instructor time, compensation, incentive, evaluation
- Materials development policies for ownership, copyright, royalty sharing
- Student enrollment, tuition and fees, payment procedures
- Joint institutional policies, including (a) accreditation, class credits, grade reporting; (b) missed classes, late papers, testing security; (c) video recording, duplicating, distributing class sessions
- Logistic process for (a) scheduling room and network facilities; (b) unlocking building and classrooms, turning on and setting up equipment; (c) developing contingency plans for canceled and/or delayed meetings

Micro Level

- Prioritize topics and activities; develop a "tight" agenda.
- Budget your time carefully; chart objectives.
- Build in extra time to set up and practice.
- Be respectful of others' *time*. Guest lecturer? Confirm, inform, assist.
- Plan, act, and follow through. Pay attention to details in advance; save time during the teleclass.
- Distribute class materials beforehand to avoid loosing minutes at class opening.
- Appoint a facilitator/leader at remote sites.
- Define facilitator/leader duties.

Designing Instruction for Learning 115

BOX 5.2. Organize Your Instruction

Estimate in minutes how much time you want to allocate to each necessary class component.

- "Housekeeping" (greetings, old business, special instructions, etc.)
- Quick review of previous materials
- Introduction to new materials: "Tell 'em what you're going to tell 'em."
- Presentation of objectives
- Instructional activities: "Tell 'em."
- Planned interaction and feedback time throughout to check understanding, learner questions, clarifications
- Hourly stretches: physical and mental breaks—time to refocus, regroup
- Wrap-up: "Tell 'em what you told 'em."
- Time for student input: short, weekly "exit evaluations" (paper and pencil, logging into BBS chat mode, or anonymous conferencing journal)

Box 5.3 illustrates a template you can use to chart your presentation.

Why Organize and Chart Your Presentation?

☆ Helpful Hints

- ☆ Interactions take longer. You need to plan, organize, and streamline content.
    - ❖ 1 hour teleteaching time = ¾ hour traditional teaching time
- ☆ Lectures go faster!
    - ❖ 1 hour teleteaching time = 1 ½ hours traditional teaching time

BOX 5.3. Charting Template: Planning an Interactive Demonstration						
Prompt	Outline	Time	Strategies	Need to:	Completed?	

☆ Try to spend 30% of class time in student-centered learning activities.

Messaging Style

Working with and observing participants in distance learning environments, we've observed that learners have to "work harder" to grasp material than they do in a face-to-face learning environment. This is because of the restrictions imposed by both the distance and the technology. For one thing, it takes extra effort to pay attention to and keep pace with the teacher. It also takes time and effort to become comfortable with the technological hardware (mics, computers, cameras) and the modifications in not only the classroom environment as a whole but, more specifically, in the students' personal workspace. A third reason that students in distance learning environments work harder is the problem of timing delays. The normal pacing of pauses that occur in face-to-face teaching environments are very hard to duplicate. So if a key point is missed or misunderstood, participants at distant sites can easily become lost. A fourth reason has to do with tension-related fatigue: eye irritation, stiff muscles from rigid postures (leaning and tensing in their intense effort to keep pace), and the tendency to stare and not blink often enough to avoid eye strain. Because of these and other alterations, learners are working harder to learn and therefore tire more quickly mentally and physically. Tiring causes attention and reten-

> **BOX 5.4. Important Elements of Messaging Style**
>
> - Your presentation skills
> - Giving and receiving feedback
> - Developing questioning strategies
> - Turning verbal information into visual communication
> - Organizing information into "manageable chunks" that can be received, understood, and remembered

tion gaps. For these reasons, the instructor's messaging style becomes very important in creating a positive learning environment. See Box 5.4 for important elements of messaging style.

Your Presentation Skills

In Chapter 4, we talked about the importance of developing good audio and video presentations skills. The checklist in Box 5.5 builds on these skills. The concepts apply to all distance learning environments.

Giving and Receiving Feedback

Your ability to give and receive feedback is an important component of open and distance education. Feedback is important because it helps to "span the distance" and complete the communications loop. Feedback is an important tool that can help you help learners stay motivated and interested. Box 5.6 presents a checklist for giving and receiving feedback.

Questioning Strategies

An important part of the communication process is getting across the idea that none of us has all the answers . . . and all of us have the questions. Therefore, planning how you will *ask* questions is as impor-

BOX 5.5. Presentation Skills

Your presentation skills checklist should include the following:

- Verbal delivery

    Voice pitch and volume (vary to avoid monotony)

    Pacing, phrasing, diction, and enunciation (Do you speak quickly? That's okay as long as you project your voice and get into the habit of pausing for a split second at natural phrase points—it lets the ear catch up and compensates for transmission "lag time")

- Relaxed body posture and positive body language

    Hands relaxed, calm gestures

    Face relaxed, animated, friendly, expressive

    Head nodding understanding

    Walking/leaning in and out of camera range

- Personal enthusiasm: draws participants into the lesson, creates atmosphere, sets example of what you expect in return
- Eye contact: encourages interaction, builds confidence
- Mannerisms

    Avoid fidgeting: use smaller, more quiet movements

- Be conscious of nonverbal cues you send and receive

    Positive cues
    - Nodding head in agreement
    - Making eye contact
    - Leaning forward in anticipation
    - Relaxed hand and face gestures

    Negative cues
    - Look of "panic"
    - "Freezing": dead silence
    - Nervous smiles
    - Fidgeting with "things"

Designing Instruction for Learning 119

BOX 5.6. Feedback Skills

Your feedback checklist should include the following:

- Pause between key points to allow time.
    - For thinking
    - For limitations of the technology

- Address participants by name.
- Have a seating chart ready to "evoke" feedback, when needed.
- Require student participation outside of class.
    - BBS activities
    - Fax assignments

- Design, collect, and respond to weekly student "exit surveys."
- Intersperse presentation with frequent use of Q & A.
- Practice sending and receiving verbal and nonverbal signals.
    - Make a "private viewing" videocassette recording of yourself.
    - Are you encouraging learners' involvement?
    - Are you maximizing learners' understanding?

---

tant as planning what you will *say* about the subject. As shown in Box 5.7, well-formed questions enhance the quality and content of the teleclass.

Direct Questions. Direct questions at frequent intervals throughout talk appear to be the best technique for ensuring understanding and attentiveness.

Functions of direct questioning include the following:

- It requires use of the subject matter to solve a problem, thereby helping to *guide participants in understanding* and *synthesize that understanding with prior experiences.*

> **BOX 5.7. When you use frequent Q & A, two things happen:**
>
> - The groups interact.
> - The learners begin to think.

- It can be used to review what's been covered so that participants can *organize and sequence their thoughts*.
- It provides the opportunity to *integrate the new information* with prior knowledge and experience.
- It keeps the presenter aware of how the group is doing.
- It keeps the group on its toes.
- It brings out areas of misunderstanding that need to be clarified.
- It causes the presenter to think through several approaches to the topic, making the speaker better prepared and the presentation more interesting.
- It gives participants cues as to how they need to study for tests.
- It is a way to handle problem participants.

Feedback Questions. Feedback questions have two important uses in participative methods: (a) to keep participants involved and (b) to check to see if participants are synthesizing material.

Some forms of feedback questions include the following:

- Tell me what I just told you. *(Show me you heard my words.)*
- In your own words, what did she say? *(Show me you have the general idea.)*
- What was the third of the five steps described? *(Show me you have an idea of the process or sequence.)*
- *Why* was that important? *(Show me you can understand the rationale.)*
- *How* does this apply? Can you use what we've covered to solve the problem of . . .? What applications does this have? *(Show me you understand both meaning and relevance.)*
- What experiences have you had that confirm? *(Show me you've grasped the meaning.)*

Your Personal Image: Working With Color

In most distance learning environments, making the right choices about clothing and accessories takes on new importance. Color, pattern, and line choices can enhance your presentation or pose a distraction to the learner(s). These problems have to do with things such as the lighting (or lack of lighting) at each site and the screen-"refreshing" process that compressed video uses to send images. You will therefore want to give a little extra thought to the way you package yourself.

The importance of the instructor's/trainer's and the learner's personal image carries over into the computer labs and automated skills labs. Learners who choose to attend lab dressed in heavy jewelry, bright white shirts, blouses with ruffles, or very tight pants/skirts, to name a few, become a distraction to themselves, their fellow learners (at their location and the distant classrooms), and the instructors/trainers. Glares from their clothing or jewelry on the computer monitor screens cause increased eye fatigue.

Another growing concern in this age of technology is the slow accumulative effect of incorrect movements that can cause mild to serious musculoskeletal injury. Tight clothing may force the learner into incorrect postures that create poor habits and lead to muscle and nerve damage over time.

In general, choose clean uncluttered lines (avoid ruffles and trendy clothing) and colors that are neither very dark (black, navy blue) or very light (white, pastels). Colors that fall in the middle range of value and intensity seem to be handled more efficiently by the camera lens and computer monitors or workstations. Slacks and skirts or dresses need to be long enough to be considered modest. The true test for correct loose fit and comfort for your clothes comes when you sit down and begin carrying on a conversation. There are some more definitive rules on color combinations that can help you choose your outfit. See Box 5.8 for hints on working with color.

More About Color. Complementary colors lie opposite each other on a color wheel: red and green, blue and orange, or yellow and violet. *Complementary colors seem to pull in opposite directions, creating a tension between them.* Believe it or not, this tension is picked up by the

> ### BOX 5.8. Working With Color
>
> ☆ **Helpful Hints**
>
> - ☆ Avoid white and black*
>   - ■ White may cause camera lens to "close down," throwing shadows across face. White can also cause "glare."
>   - ■ Black may cause camera lens to "open up," washing out facial features and expressions.
>
>   *Exception: Okay if worn with contrasting colors close to face (scarves, ties)
>
> - ☆ Avoid pastels: They have the same effect as white.
> - ☆ Avoid "neons": They produce both glare and distraction.
> - ☆ Avoid large or small prints of complementary colors.**
>
>   ** Large or small prints are okay if they are of equal value and intensity and if they are analogous, triadic, or monochromatic.

cameras as they try to adjust to the opposing fields. These phenomena can cause a blurring of the image—especially true for compressed video and personal computer (PC)-based Internet transmissions.

Analogous, triadic, and monochromatic combinations create a harmonious effect due to the close relationship between the hues. In these combinations, you don't find the tension produced by complementary color schemes. Therefore, there is less chance of screen blurring.

- Analogous colors: colors next to each other on the wheel
- Triadic colors: colors equidistant from each other on the wheel (works best when colors selected have same depth and hue)
- Monochromatic colors: different intensities of the same color—dark, medium, and light blue

We began this section by asking the question, "When it comes to teaching in distance learning environments, what things are different?"

TABLE 5.2 What Is Different: Preparing Yourself

Item Variable	Audio	Video	Computer	Multimodel
Organizing your time [Attention]	X	XX	X	XX
Working with equipment [Confidence]	X	XX	XX	XX
Organizing instruction [Relevance]	X	X	X	XX
Your messaging style [Confidence, Satisfaction]	X	XX	X	X
Project a positive image [Confidence, Satisfaction]	X	XX	LS	X
Use of participative methods and techniques [Attention, Relevance Confidence, Satisfaction]	LS	X	LS	X

NOTE: Under each column heading, we have placed an X if the concept discussed requires a different emphasis in that delivery system as it is in a traditional teaching/training environment. Some entries have a XX (double X), which means that the differences are multifaceted and therefore require a different emphasis for their various parts. LS stands for "level specific," indicating that depending on the specific distance learning delivery tool, the characteristics might or might not be the same as in a traditional learning environment.

In most cases, you'll find that it's more a matter of a difference in emphasis in how you approach teaching than how you construct your basic teaching design. One way to address these differences in emphasis is to think in terms of preparing yourself, your materials, and your students. We have just finished our discussion on preparing yourself for distance teaching/training, in which we focused on these four areas: organizing your time, organizing your instruction, sharpening your message style, and projecting a positive image. We are now ready to summarize these differences with the following visual representation.

As in the previous section, where we discussed and summarized those things that remain the same when you make the transition from traditional teaching and learning environments to distance teaching/learning environments, we've listed for you the various distance learning delivery methods you may be involved with (see Table 5.2). Under each column heading, we have placed an X if the concept discussed requires a different emphasis in that delivery system than in a traditional teaching/training environment. Some entries have a XX (double X), which means that the differences are multifaceted and therefore require a different emphasis for their various parts. As in our earlier example, LS stands for level specific, indicating that depending on the specific distance learning delivery tool, the characteristics might or might not be the same as in a traditional learning environment.

 THE QUESTION:

What do you mean by "participative teaching methods and techniques"?

☞ THE ANSWER:

Participative teaching methods incorporate techniques that grab and maintain learner attention, show relevance to learner needs, and incorporate communication and feedback elements that build learner confidence and satisfaction (ARCS).

Earlier in this section, we talked about the relationship between meaningful learning and learner participation, interaction, and/or involvement. No matter which term is used, the point we made was that an important relationship *does exist* between meaningful learning and the extent to which learners are involved in *what* is taught and *how* it's taught. This relationship is especially important to consider in distance education, where the dynamics of teaching and learning as we know them have changed and both teacher and learner may feel temporarily "out of sync" functioning in the different environment.

As we add the attributes of the distance education technologies to the equation, we see that there are areas where a *difference in emphasis* on how we prepare to teach will help to span the distance, assist learners in maintaining high levels of participation, and ensure our goal of providing meaningful learning.

On the following pages, we will discuss how the most widely used form of instruction, the lecture, can be effectively used in open and distance learning environments.

The Participative Lecture

Educational studies tell us that nearly two thirds of all adult classroom learning situations use the lecture method. So it is realistic to say that the lecture can and will be a teaching method of choice for many distance educators. The most effective teleteaching lectures go beyond the "I talk, you listen" process, taking the form of a *participative lecture*. Participative lectures actively involve learners in the learner process at several levels:

- Talking
- Writing
- "Watching for"
- Thinking
- Doing

As we stated earlier, participative lectures incorporate techniques that grab and maintain learner attention, show relevance to learner needs, and incorporate communication and feedback elements that build learner confidence and satisfaction (ARCS).

The following scenario will give you an idea of how one instructor, preparing for an interactive video class, incorporated these participative elements into his standard lecture format.

Scenario. Dr. Jones is a professor in the College of Medicine. He is teaching an intermediate-level course for paramedics in the local community. Dr. Jones has taught this course in the same way (traditional lecture format with lab) for 10 years. His students are typically between the ages of 18 and 38, with a high school education plus 2 years of advanced coursework. By nature, his students are compulsive and action oriented; they "think on their feet," thrive under pressure, and get great satisfaction from knowing the answers and making the right decisions. Students are used to having the professor "right there" and to being constantly stimulated and motivated.

Dr. Jones has decided that the lecture method is the best teaching choice, based on the attributes of the learner and the nature of the materials to be taught. He has the knowledge/information that the students do not. Furthermore, the students have not had experiences to draw from that will allow them to efficiently discover the knowledge/

information. If such a base of experience did exist, Dr. Jones may have chosen group discussion or case study teaching methods. Without that critical base of knowledge to draw from, the more formal lecture method is the most appropriate choice.

Preparing the Participative Lecture. To help the students at the local and remote sites maintain their focus and interest, and to avoid the confusion that could occur without having an instructor physically present in the room, Dr. Jones carefully plans and prepares each element of his lecture. To begin with, he clearly states the learning objectives, limits major points to no more than three to five per hour, and incorporates interactive learning strategies throughout the lecture, such as pauses for planned question and answer segments and "mini" student reports. In addition, Dr. Jones uses a variety of presentation techniques within the lecture. For example, instead of giving a lecture on all points, he may choose a minilecture (7-10 minutes) to communicate the first point. To communicate the second point, Dr. Jones decides to use a video segment (5-7 minutes), complete with preassigned instructions to learners—for example, items to look for and examples of concepts discussed. To present the third learning objective, Dr. Jones shifts the responsibility for teaching/learning to the students via preassigned homework in which a student has been assigned to demonstrate findings from a remote location. To bring the class to closure, Dr. Jones had previously invited a colleague from an out-of-state university to join the class on-line from yet another remote site and to present the summary and conclusions to the evening's lecture. What Dr. Jones has done in this scenario, then, is transform a traditional lecture into a participative lecture by combining techniques from other common teaching methods to vary the presentation and enhance the learning process.

Something to think about: You are in the lecture mode not only when you are the primary focus of the class through talking. You can also be in a lecture mode when you are

Designing Instruction for Learning   127

* ❖ *narrating information,*
* ❖ *giving information in written form, and*
* ❖ *conveying the bulk of information through charts, slides, transparencies, or movies.*

Engaging Distance Learners

Through the years, engaging learners has been considered the key to success in traditional classroom teaching models. Recent studies have found that the interaction caused by engaging students is also the key to success in distance education.

The following section discusses learning strategies that engage distance learners and prepare them to learn.

 THE QUESTION:

How do I prepare students to learn from a distance?

☞ THE ANSWER:

Create a sense of "readiness" by:

◆ Educating and preparing students for the new experience.
◆ Setting up strong communication and information channels.

Students participating in the teleclass—at both the local and remote sites—quickly find that the teaching and learning conditions they are used to have changed. So have other familiar experiences, such as classroom dynamics and access to the instructor—before, during, and after class. Students, therefore, can feel isolated and alone.

> **BOX 5.9. Six weeks before class:**
>
> - Set up lines of communications: phone/fax/electronic bulletin boards (BBS).
> - Construct list of all contact numbers (phone/fax/BBS) to all local and remote students and facilitators.

Educate and Prepare Students

- About the new teaching/learning environment
- About the advantages/disadvantages
- About what they can expect/cannot expect from you and the environment
- About what you expect/do not expect of them
- About why participation and interaction are important
- About the ground rules, policies, and procedures
- About what it feels like to teach from a distance

Communications and Information Sharing Planning

The teaching/learning conditions that students are used to have changed. So have the group dynamics. So have students' ability to "access" the instructor (before, during, after class). Students can easily feel isolated. You can eliminate some of the potential problems by establishing good lines of communication well before class begins. Boxes 5.9, 5.10, and 5.11 present some ideas that have helped other distance instructors and distance learners.

These activities may seem time intensive, but the investment will pay off.

☆ More ideas for creating good lines of communication

- ☆ Teach a class from the remote site.
- ☆ Bring remote classes to main campus for work weekends.

> **BOX 5.10. Two weeks before class:**
>
> Send students and facilitator a supplementary communications and information packet of materials that includes the following:
>
> - Instructor, facilitator/preceptor, students' names, telephone and fax numbers, e-mail addresses
> - Description of the distance learning environment
> - Contingency plans (audioconference bridging procedure and telephone number, BBS "chat" mode instructions, library videotape viewing/group study instructions, etc.)
> - CBT (computer-based training) disks that correspond to textbook readings and assignments.
> - A short biography of yourself and all students before class begins

☆ Informally meet with all groups at a central location for a fun time.
☆ Set up lines of communications (phone/fax/BBS).
☆ Each week, focus class activities around a remote site and the students there.

Students will see that you are aware of the changes you are going through and that you are attempting to create a healthy learning environment. Eventually, these activities will also establish a sense of community among all sites, as students learn to work together and themselves contribute to "spanning the distance."

Create a Sense of "Readiness"

There's no getting around it. The planning and preparation it takes to prepare learners takes time and effort. Be patient. Your efforts

> **BOX 5.11. Two or three days before class:**
>
> - Send students a brief letter reminding them of class date and time. Outline objectives, goals, special instructions, etc.
> - Direct students to come to class prepared with three questions or ideas related to the topic, objectives (15-20 minute activity). Keep letter short with plenty of space for responses.
>
> **During first class:**
>
> - Create a photo library of all students, at all sites
> - Develop seating chart of all students, at all sites

will pay off if you take time to prepare for the activities listed in Box 5.12.

With this, we finish our discussion on "preparing your students" for distance teaching/training, in which we focused on preparing students to learn by creating a sense of readiness. We are now ready to begin our summary of the section.

As in the previous summary sections, we've created a matrix of the various distance learning delivery methods with the strategies for engaging distance learners (see Table 5.3). Under each column heading, we have placed an X if the concept discussed requires a different emphasis in that delivery system than in a traditional teaching/training environment. Some entries have a XX (double X), which means that the differences are multifaceted and therefore require a different emphasis for their various parts. As in our earlier example, LS stands for Level Specific, indicating that depending on the specific distance learning delivery tool, the characteristics might or might not be the same as in a traditional learning environment.

Designing Instruction for Learning 131

> ## BOX 5.12. Aggressively plan for student involvement!
>
> - Get students involved *early!*
> - *Set the example!* Establish interactive routines.
> - *Your* efforts to communicate and "span the distance" will affect *their* efforts to communicate and "span the distance."
> - Weave interactive teaching techniques through teaching method (Q & A, group discussions, etc.).
> - Adapt message style: Deliver information in short, manageable "chunks," alternated with learning activities that engage students (buzz groups, demonstrations, etc.).

TABLE 5.3 What Is Different: Preparing Your Students

Item Variable	*Audio*	*Video*	*Computer*	*Multimodel*
Preparing students to learn				
Educate and inform	X	X	X	X
Communications and information links	LS	X	LS	X
Contingency planning	LS	X	LS	X
Rules, policies, procedures	X	XX	LS	XX
Creating "readiness":				
Engaging distance learners				
Agendas, objectives	LS	X	LS	X
Visual cues	LS	X	LS	X
Interactive study guides	XX	LS	LS	X
Enhancing learning: "manageable chunks"	X	LS	LS	XX
Enhancing learning: reinforce for retention	X	X	X	XX
Enhancing learning: variety of activities	LS	X	LS	X
Enhancing learning: develop direct questioning and feedback skills	LS	LS	X	X

NOTE: Under each column heading, we have placed an X if the concept discussed requires a different emphasis in that delivery system as it is in a traditional teaching/training environment. Some entries have a XX (double X), which means that the differences are multifaceted and therefore require a different emphasis for their various parts. LS stands for "level specific," indicating that depending on the specific distance learning delivery tool, the characteristics might or might not be the same as in a traditional learning environment.

Selecting Teachers for Distance Learning

SCENARIO

You are the director of distance learning activities. You are in the process of introducing two-way interactive video to teach educational technology students how to develop computer-assisted instruction (CAI).

YOUR TASK

- Where do you begin?
- What "criteria" will you look for?
- How can you enhance the teaching of the following kinds of students?
  - Willing and able
  - Willing and not so able
  - Unwilling but "drafted"

DISCUSSION . . .

Creating Meaningful Lesson Plans for Open and Distance Learning

SCENARIO

You will be teaching from a distance using [choose from audiographics, PC-based BBS, and two-way interactive video]. You have two learners at one remote site, three learners at another, and four learners with you at the local site.

YOUR TASK

Create a lesson plan that will provide meaningful learning to both sets of students—distant and face-to-face.

DISCUSSION . . .

*Using Technology to Broaden Your Horizons . . .
and Your Learners' Horizons*

SCENARIO

You will have access to PC-based interactive video desktop units for your distance learning courses this year. The multifunctional units also allow you to access information from your local area network (LAN), the Internet, and your colleagues around the world.

YOUR TASK:

Structure a teaching plan that will make use of the technology and at the same time make students aware of the broad range of resources and ideas they can tap into.

CHAPTER **6**

Turning Verbal Information Into Visual Communication

The information in Chapter 6 will help you as you begin to turn verbal information into visual communications, including ideas on these topics:

- Working with space

- Working with text and fonts

- Visual relationships: working with color, line, and graphics

Working with and observing participants in distance learning environments, we've observed that learners have to "work a little harder" to grasp material than they do in a face-to-face learning environment. Following are some reasons for this:

- The technology can be distracting.
- The field of vision is limited (from 3-dimensional to 2-dimensional).
- Eye contact can be difficult to make.
- Participants can get "lost."

It is therefore important to design clear, easy-to-follow graphics that not only help gain and maintain participants' interest but that also make the technology transparent, shifting the focus from the technology to the learning process. This process begins with your ability to turn verbal information into visual communication. As you go through a sequence of information, you should constantly ask yourself, How can I visualize this? In other words, along with deciding *what* you will say, you need to consider *how* you will say it:

- Look for ways to illustrate ideas.
- Use pictures instead of words.
- Number graphics for easy identification.
- Use graphics to reinforce learning.
- Design visuals to maximize viewer participation.
- Present questions and problems in graphic form.
- Use color, shape, location, and size for contrast.
- Focus attention through line boxes, shadow, boxes.

The next few pages are packed with ideas for designing graphics and materials for open and distance learning environments. You will *definitely* want to keep these within reach!

Working With Space

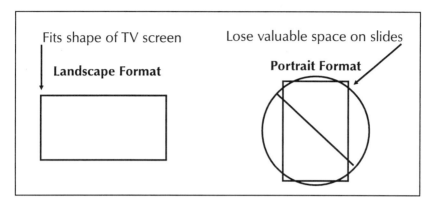

Computer and television screens are set in a "landscape" format, with a 3 × 4 aspect ratio. That means for every 3 three units of measurement down, there are 4 units across so that the page is wider than it is tall. In our everyday work, we are used to presenting material in a "portrait" format, having an aspect ratio of about 3 × 2 so that the page is taller than it is wide. With portrait format, there is wasted space on each side, and the materials at the top and bottom of the page are not as easily seen.

Reformatting hard copy materials to landscape format will give you better use of the teleteaching screen for distance learning environments using telematics, interactive video, and on-line computer formats.

How does this fit with your experience?

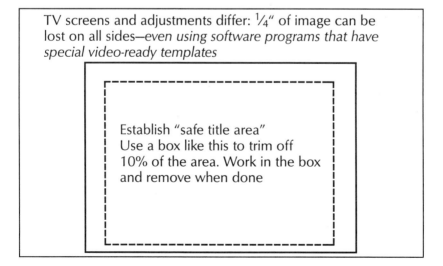

In this example, we are working with the parameters set by a popular computer presentation program. The program set up the areas to fit a presentation given via computer. Note that all software presentations default to a landscape format. However, many programs don't adjust for transfer from digital computer formats to analog video formats—where approximately ¼" all round can get lost in the process. Therefore, it is best to create your own "safe title area" within the given parameters to compensate for moving a presentation from a computer screen to a video screen.

An easy way to do this is to set up your presentation within the safe title area:

1. Find the master slide template (in Microsoft Powerpoint, for example, you would go to the top tool bar, choose "View," then "Master," then "Slide Master").
2. Draw a brightly colored box on the Slide Master—one that greatly contrasts with the background of your presentation. The reason for the contrasting color is so you won't forget to remove the box when you complete the presentation!
3. Adjust all text and graphics to fit within the box.
4. Go back to the master slide template when you have finished presentation and delete the box.

Word Processing
"Safe Title Area"

Option #1
❖ Set 2" margins all around
❖ Select 18-point **bold** font
❖ Set spacing to 1 ½"

You can get the same effect—creating a safe title area—with a word processor by using Options 1 or 2 shown here:

WORD PROCESSING

Option #2

- ❖ Select "column" setting
- ❖ Choose 2 columns
- ❖ Line spacing: 1 ½" space
- ❖ 7 × 7 rule
- ❖ Triple space between 7 × 7s

WORKING WITH SPACE

- ❖ 5 words in the title
- ❖ MAX: 7 lines in height ⟶ 7 × 7 rule
- ❖ MAX: 7 words in width ⟶

For best readability:

- ♦ Limit title to five words.
- ♦ Observe 7 × 7 Rule—7 lines per slide, 7 words per line.

How does this fit with your experience?

Working With Texts and Fonts

Sans Serif Fonts

Choose simple sans serif fonts—**bold** type. Sans serif letters are clean, crisp units. **Bold** type adds to the sharpness of the letters.

Video compression processes bold sans serif fonts easily, so remote sites receive clean, readable images.

Arial
Britain Bold
Palatino
Tahoma

Working With Text and Fonts
Serif Fonts

Serif fonts can cause screen blurring. This is because of the little "feet" at the end of each letter designed to lead our eyes

r i f
↑ ↑ ↑

Times New Roman
Book Antiqua
Courier New

The video compression process is constantly "refreshing the screen." It looks for lines. It sees the little feet as random pixels, not lines, and becomes confused, causing the screen to shimmer and blur.

Working With Text and Fonts
 Rules of Thumb

- ❖ Simple sans serif fonts
- ❖ Bold letters
- ❖ Upper- and lowercase letters
  (ALL CAPS IS HARD TO READ)

Working With Text and Fonts
 Rules of Thumb for Readability

- ❖ Left aligned "bullets"
- ❖ Off-center graphics
- ❖ Keep it simple, clean, easy
- ❖ AVOID ALL CAPS
- ❖ Upper- and lowercase letters
- ❖ Formal: Cap Key Words
- ❖ Informal: Cap first word only

Visual Relationships:
Working With Color, Line, and Graphics

WORKING WITH COLORS:
CREATIVE

Some people feel that dark text on light background is most readable.

Black or navy on white, yellow, or blue

Others feel that light text on dark background is easier on the eye.

White, yellow, orange, or aqua on purple, blue, green, or black

Whichever you prefer, the key is to use colors that are deeply contrasting in value and intensity.

Follow same guidelines for diagrams and drawings . . .

WORKING WITH COLORS:
CREATIVE

 Rules of Thumb
- Use contrasting colors.
- Use red as an accent color.

WORKING WITH COLORS:
CREATIVE

Did you know . . .
- 1 of every 10 people has a visual color deficiency.
- The most common deficiency: *red and green.*

Use red as an accent color only.
- TVs have a hard time reproducing red.
- Red "bleeds" into surrounding colors, making them motley and greyed in appearance.

WORKING WITH COLORS:
TECHNICAL

❖ Problems with heavily dithered colors and patterns

❖ Pick up random pixels of black and red fill

◆ Random pixels cause screen flicker

◆ Colors appear dark and dingy

WORKING WITH LINES

❖ Line widths of 1 pixel cause screen flicker

❖ Line widths of 3 pixels or more are suggested

This is an important point, because of the difference in the way a computer generates lines and the video displays lines. Every line, every object a computer generates, is created by laying down tiny pixels from left to right across the screen. Pixels have jagged edges. Also, sometimes the computer skips a pixel. The area is so small that we can't see the skipped pixel with our naked eye. In the case of a thin line, it still looks like an unbroken line. But to the video monitor, which is continually scanning the screen, looking for unbroken lines, the tiny break in pattern could cause slight screen flutter that can slightly blur the picture. Therefore, using thick lines and bold letters of at least 3 pixel widths will help ensure unbroken lines and, therefore, clearer transmission of data.

More Tips for Developing Graphics . . .

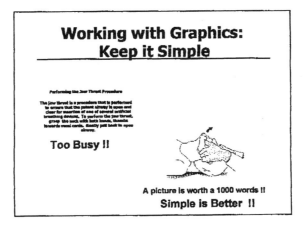

We have just finished our discussion on preparing your materials for open and distance teaching/training, in which we focused on these areas:

- Presentation graphics and materials design
- Topography and space
- Text, fonts, and visual relationships
- Color, line, graphics

We are now ready to summarize these differences as they apply to the various open and distance learning technologies and environments. As in the previous summary sections, we've created a matrix of the various distance learning delivery methods with techniques for developing and designing presentation materials (see Table 6.1). Under each column heading, we have placed an X if the concept discussed requires a different emphasis in that delivery system than in a traditional teaching/training environment. Some entries have a XX (double X), which means that the differences are multifaceted and therefore require a different emphasis for their various parts. As in our earlier example, LS stands for level specific, indicating that depending on the specific distance learning delivery tool, the characteristics might or might not be the same as in a traditional learning environment.

TABLE 6.1 What Is Different: Preparing Your Materials

Item Variable	Audio	Video	Computer	Multimodel
Prepare graphics and materials	LS	XX	LS	XX
Transfer from visual to verbal	LS	X	X	X
Transfer from verbal to visual	—	X	X	X
Transfer from written to verbal	LS	LS	LS	XX
Transfer from verbal to written	LS	X	X	XX
Transfer from visual to written	LS	X	X	X
Transfer from written to visual	—	XX	LS	XX
Time invested in technology transfer	LS	LS	LS	LS
Time invested: Months required from concept to delivery	2M	6M	6M	8M

NOTE: Standard industry ratio for first-time reformatting: 8 hours of development per 1 hour of presentation. Standard industry ratio for subsequent reformatting: 5 hours of development per 1 hour of presentation.

Glossary of Terms

Sources for selected definitions used here include Duning, Van Kekerix, and Zaborowski (1993); Hobbs (1994); Newton (1991); Portway and Lane (1992); Tele-Systems Associates (1994); and West, Farmer, and Wolff (1991).

Advanced organizer: An advanced organizer is a bridge, a transition statement, which is not only a summary of prior learning prerequisite to new material but is also a brief outline of the new material. The advanced organizer is unique among learning strategies in that, generally, students cannot be expected to create advanced organizers. This is the task of the designer or instructor.

Analog: In the United States, a single frame of video seen on broadcast television consists of 525 lines of information, placed close enough together to create a single image. By transmitting 30 of these images per second, the illusion of "full-motion video" is achieved. This system, called analog video, requires a great deal of space, or "bandwidth," to transmit the video information to the receiving set, or TV monitor.

Analog vs. digital video: Until a few years ago, analog video was the only choice and could not be easily manipulated. Recently, however, the television industry has developed a device that translates, or "codes," an analog video signal into its digital equivalent, enabling virtually the same information to be transmitted at several different frame rates and resolution levels, with predictable savings and trade-offs. The lower the resolution and frame rate, the less "bandwidth" required and the greater the savings, but the poorer the quality.

Asynchronous: Asynchronous literally means "not synchronous." In telecommunications *asynchronous transmission* refers to data transmission in which there is no clocking signal; therefore, data can be sent at irregular intervals. In distance education applications, *asynchronous* is used to refer to interactions that are not "clocked"—not sent and received at the same time. An example of asynchronous transmission would be sending electronic mail: the party receiving the e-mail message does not have to be present at the time the message is sent. The message is "posted" for later retrieval.

Audio bridge: A synonym for *bridge*—an electronic device that interconnects three or more locations, usually over telephone lines.

Audioconferencing: Interactive audio communications between or among individuals or groups at two or more locations.

Audiographics: Using lines such as telephone (audio lines) to move data to another location where the data are converted to graphics.

Audio telecommunication: A term used to identify audioconferencing.

Backbone: Backbone refers to the copper cable, fiber-optic cable, coaxial cable, and/or microwave facilities required to carry signals from town to town. In the case of telephone companies, signals would be routed from a switch in one central office to another central office some miles away. For microwave, it would be transmitted from tower to tower. *Only satellite technology, a direct site-to-site application, avoids the use of a backbone (unless you consider the satellite itself as performing that function).* Satellite technologies are often used in rural areas as a "bypass" delivery method, where a lack of fiber-optic cable in the "last mile" would otherwise make delivery of distance education technologies impossible.

Bandwidth: The difference between the lowest and the highest frequencies that designated channels for communications are capable of carrying. Broader bandwidths carry greater amounts of information.

Bridge: An internetworking device that connects three or more locations, similar local area networks running on like protocols, connected over an electronic device (bridge); frequently, the connection for audio communication is carried over the telephone lines.

Bridging: The actual act of making the electronic connection, most often over telephone lines, between a number of points at various locations.

Broadcast signal: One-direction transmitted information made available to an unspecified audience.

Capital equipment budget: A budget that includes planning for larger durable items, including audiovisual and other electronic hardware. The actual complete plan may be segmented into phases across more than one budget year.

Chunking: This concept comprises a large assortment of organizing strategies. These strategies enable the rational ordering, classifying, or arranging of complex arrays. They aid persons in intellectual management of large amounts of data or events. These organizational strategies are preparatory in nature and, when used, are likely to aid comprehension.

Compressed video: Compressed video television signals are transmitted with much less than the usual bit rate. Full standard coding or broadcast quality television typically requires 45 to 90 megabits per second. Compressed video includes signals from 3 megabits per second (Mb/s) down to 56 kilobits per second (Kb/s). The lower bit rates typically involve some compromise in picture quality, particularly when there is rapid motion on the screen.

Computer-assisted design: Projects or sections of projects completed on computer that include design.

Computer-assisted instruction: Computer-based educational program or lesson developed with an instructor's assistance in which the learner(s) interacts with the material while using a computer.

Computer-based telecommunications system: One telecommunication system that uses as its platform computers for processing uplinking and downlinking, transmitting, and processing information.

Dedicated system: A specific system, like a telecommunications system, designated for that sole purpose. It may be set to run continuously 24 hours a day.

Direct broadcast satellite: A satellite that has a specific task identified for communications that includes transmitting video signals directly to a receiver system.

Distance education: Distance education in the United States is historically rooted in correspondence study, dating back to the 1880s (Froke, 1991). Distance education today includes these practices but has expanded to keep pace with today's technological advances. Recent distance education systems include combinations such as two-way interactive audio/video/computer-based technologies.

Distance education networks: These networks consist of four major components—backbone, last mile, terminals, and interactive video room equipment.

Downlink dish/receiver: The ground-level equipment set to receive the signals from a communications satellite.

Educational telecommunications system: A unit organized to contain the hardware, software (includes the directions for operating the hardware), at least one transport system that allows the communication of information from point to point, and the personnel who will plan, implement, manage, use, and evaluate the system.

Electronic mail (e-mail): Written word messages and/or documents transmitted electronically over a network between two individuals in two separate work centers. The e-mail may travel between two workers in one building or between individuals across a city, country, or hemisphere.

Facsimile: An image (word, picture, and/or graph) transmission system. The image is scanned in at the origination point to a transmitter. It is sent over phone lines to a receiving location where it is reconstructed into the original image on paper.

Fiber-optic cable: The introduction of fiber-optic cable during the past decade has revolutionized "wired" signal networking around the world. A tiny strand of clear fiber can transmit a hundred full-motion video signals simultaneously, taking the place of huge bundles of conventional twisted copper pairs of telephone lines. Although not available everywhere, fiber-optic cable is the "medium of choice" for most video, voice, and data applications, particularly in point-to-point situations.

Fiber-optic system: Another type of telecommunications system, it moves or transmits signals by sending pulsating beam or beams of light over a network of glass fiber.

Formative evaluation: The purpose of formative evaluation is to suggest ways of strengthening a course or program while it is being conducted. Formative evaluation is involved every time you use what you have learned about learners to determine strategy.

FM broadcast station multiplexing: Radio signals unique in themselves by the way their frequencies are modulated to allow simultaneous transmission of multiple signals.

Gateway: A device used to connect different computer networks using different communications architectures.

Interactive compressed video room equipment: The marketplace has become more competitive with new products every few months. Digital equipment pricing has finally reached parity with analog, but application continues to be a constant problem. Typically, compressed video networks run at 768 Kb/s or less. Video teleconferencing systems that rely on substantial compression (less than 768 Kb/s for video and audio) often reduce the performance of the audio to conserve bandwidth. The results are limited dynamic range, frequency response, and audio delays. These factors can be distracting in multiple-site sessions and may make it difficult to effectively present some material, such as foreign language classes. Still, compressed video is the most cost-effective delivery system and has proven successful for many applications in education, government, manufacturing, financial services, and medicine.

Interactive educational telecommunications system: The system established for the purpose of allowing two-way or greater communications between users (e.g., learner/instructor). Most often, this communication occurs in real time but may be set up for a delayed time for the receiving individuals to participate.

Interactive videodisc system: Computer-assisted instruction that uses videodiscs that can be designed to allow rapid, on the spot, changes in the lesson delivery (pace, direction, level of difficulty, etc.) based on the learner/student input to the system.

Interactivity: Because interaction implies a mutual or reciprocal action or influence between two or more parties, any interactive linkage, network, or device is one that permits such reciprocal action—usually (but not always) in real time.

Internet: A global collection of networks and communication interconnected through bridges, routers, or gateways.

Internetworking: Communicating between and among devices located across numerous networks.

Land-based lines and facilities: Telecommunications systems that transmit by use of land-based technology and facilities.

Last mile: Last mile refers to the distance between the backbone facility and the actual customer receiving site. In the case of telephone, it would be the facility interconnecting the telco "central office" with the given community site. In rural areas, last-mile construction has proven to be a major hurdle to the development of interactive video networks. Telcos customarily charge 100% of the cost to extend fiber from the central office to the receiving site. In small rural communities where the central office is often less than a mile from the receiving site, the sum could be $10,000 to $30,000 plus a monthly maintenance fee.

Local area network (LAN): A communications network that physically joins or links communication devices such as computers together and frequently joins them to mainframes in a small area. Typically, a LAN is configured in a bus, ring, or tree topology.

Media service center (multimedia support center): A designated section or support unit in an organization directed to assist with audio, video, and other multimedia technologies, including but not limited to computer technologies and applications.

Modeling: Computers and their applications used to create various levels of real-life representations of situations, tasks, or objects.

Modem: A device used to convert the digital data it receives into the needed analog signal for transmission over one of the telecommunications lines and likewise it converts the analog signals it receives over to data for reading by the receiver.

Multimodel design: The application or blending of more than one technique or technology to address a project or situation, such as distance education or distance learning.

On-demand system: An educational telecommunications system set up to operate at specific times when there are students/learners or other request for its use.

Glossary of Terms 153

Operating lifetime: A length of time that research and/or experience has shown to be the average time that a device or system will operate reliably at a given use rate.

Origination site: The location from which the activity or program is carried out or transmitted.

Program budget: A listing of the expenditures and income for a single activity. It may include very detailed line-by-line information about the activity's expenses and income generated or it may be in a summary.

Receiving equipment: The equipment located at the downlink point where the communication is accepted, processed, and presented as a program or other learning activity.

Receive site: The location or point where the activity or program communication reception occurs.

Redundancy: The deliberate and systematic duplication within a telecommunications system for the express purpose of protecting against primary telecommunication system major malfunctions or failure.

Ring: One of the LAN topologies. In this design, the workstations are connected in a closed loop like a train track set. The users enter data into their communications device, or computer, and the data are transmitted in only one direction around the ring. The data can be then read by all stations on the loop.

Satellite communications: The age of communications satellites, placed in geosynchronous orbit above the earth's equator, eliminated much of the need for land-based microwave networks, because a single "uplink" could transmit a signal back down to earth. Most domestic satellites have a "conus footprint," which means the signal can be picked up by a receive dish anywhere in the continental United States. Because broadcasting to thousands of sites costs the same as broadcasting to one site, satellite communications have become the most cost-effective point-to-mass technologies to date, and many national distributors of live and pretaped programs use satellite broadcasts to distribute their programs.

Sending equipment: Telecommunication hardware and software located at the originating site for the purpose of projecting/sending a program signal to the designated reception sites.

Sequencing: Sequencing means to divide appropriate information into steps and stages that will help learners understand and retain materials. Possible types of sequencing include topic-by-topic, chronological, place-to-place, concentric circles, and problem-centered sequencing.

Simulation and gaming: Teaching techniques that model an event, procedure, or skill by imitating it or replicating it. The learner/student is involved with a high level of interaction as he or she applies strategies and/or decision making to the scenarios.

Slow-scan television: A telecommunication technology using the telephone that captures still-frame pictures and displays them on television monitors.

Synchronous transmission: Synchronous transmission refers to the fixed transmission of data between sender and receiver. In distance education, the term *synchronous* is used to refer to interactions that are "clocked"—that is, interactions that must be sent and received at the same time. An example of a synchronous distance education application is computer-mediated conferencing (CMC): The person initiating the conference expects to interact electronically in real time with a person or persons at various sites.

T1 and DS3 telephone lines: Some of the slower frame rates can be transmitted over single telephone lines. Near full-motion picture quality images can be transmitted over bundles of telephone lines (called T1 lines). At its fastest frame rate and resolution (DS3 rate), the digital signal is considered the equivalent of an analog signal and requires bandwidth that approaches the bandwidth required to transmit analog video.

Telecommunications: Telecommunications is defined in Newton's *Telecom Dictionary* (1991) as the art and science of communicating over a distance by telephone, telegraph, and radio.

Teleconferencing: Teleconferencing combines the prefix *tele* and the word *conferencing*, with tele meaning "at a distance" and conferencing implying a meeting. Therefore, the combined word, *teleconferencing*, is used to describe "meeting at a distance." In the United States, the word teleconferencing has become a generic term for all kinds of meetings conducted via communication technology. The word *video* is added to teleconferencing or conferencing (videoconferencing) to describe meeting at a distance, using two-way audio and video communication (Portway & Lane, 1992).

Terminal emulation: When computers have the ability to operate like another type of terminal linked on a network or to another processing unit.

Terminal equipment: This equipment is used to transmit and receive video, audio, and data signals to and from other sites. CODECs (coders-decoders) are used for digital video on copper or fiber networks. Laser-based terminals are used for linear broadband (analog) video fiber applications together with modulators and demodulators, which are also used for coaxial cable.

Topology: The interconnections of end points or stations to networks. Frequently used topologies include ring, bus, and tree.

Transmission equipment: Various types of telecommunications hardware and software used to transmit signal to the reception location(s).

Uplink: The equipment located where the telecommunication signals originate. It may include signal dishes, fiber-optic, or other communications lines in addition to other electronic equipment used, for example, to transmit the signal to a communications satellite.

Video telecommunications system: One- or two-way telecommunications systems with the capability to transmit or transmit and receive video signals of full motion or lesser quality type between sites.

Video teleconferencing: The real-time, and usually two-way, interactive transmission of digitized video images between two or more locations is called video teleconferencing or teleconferencing. Teleconferencing requires a wideband transmission facility. Transmitted images may be freeze-frame (in which the television screen is repainted every few seconds to every 20 seconds) or full motion. Bandwidth requirements for two-way videoconferencing range from 6 MHz for analog, full-motion, full-color, commercial grade TV to two 56 Kb/s lines for digitally encoded reasonably full-motion, full-color to 1,544 Mb/s for very good quality, full-color, full-motion TV.

Voice: A telecommunication system able to transmit two-way audio communication alone or in combination with other content, such as written data, one- or two-way video, and so on.

VSAT (very small aperture terminal): VSAT refers to a relatively small satellite antenna, typically 1.5 to 3.0 meters in diameter, used for transmitting and receiving data communications. You often see VSATs on top of retail stores, which use them for transmitting data. More recently, VSATs are being used to transmit compressed video signals.

References

American Society for Training and Development. (1974). *ASTD training and development manual.* Madison, WI: Author.

American Society for Training and Development. (1976). *ASTD training and development manual* (Updated). Madison, WI: Author.

American Society for Training and Development. (1978). *A study of professional training and development competencies and roles.* Madison, WI: Author.

Ausubel, D. P., Novak, J. D., & Hanesian, H. (1978). *Educational psychology: A cognitive view.* New York: Holt, Rinehart & Winston.

Brookfield, S. (1984). *Understanding and facilitating adult learning.* San Francisco: Jossey-Bass.

Civil Service Commission. (1975-76). Washington, DC: Author.

Dillon, C., Hengst, H., & Zoller, D. (1991). Instructional strategies and student involvement in distance education: A study of the Oklahoma Televised Instruction System. *American Journal of Distance Education, 6*(1) 28-41.

Duning, B. S., Van Kekerix, M. J., & Zaborowski, L. M. (1993). *Reaching learners through telecommunications.* San Francisco: Jossey-Bass.

Egan, M., Welch, M., Page, B., & Sebastian, J. (1991). *Effective television teaching: Perceptions of those who count most . . . distance learners.* Salt Lake City: University of Utah.

Fossum, T. W., Ruoff, W. W., Rushton, W. T., Willard, M. D., Paprock, K. E., & Palmer, R. H. (1991). Identifying clinical teaching patterns and needs: An exercise in departmental self awareness. *Journal of Veterinary Medicine Education, 18*(2), 49-55.

Froke, M. (1991). *Notes on distance education*. Unpublished manuscript, Pennsylvania State University, American Center for the Advancement of Distance Education, University Park.

Graham, E. (1992, May 18). Classrooms without walls. *Wall Street Journal*, p. 1.

Hobbs, V. M. for McRel (Mid-Continent Regional Educational Laboratory. (1994). *Distance learning via fiber optic technology*. Report to the Office of Educational Research and Improvement (OERI), Department of Education (Contract #91-002-005). Washington, DC: Department of Education.

Hunt, D. E. (1971). *Matching models in education*. Toronto: Ontario Institute for Studies in Education.

Joyce, B. R. (1983). Dynamic disequilibrium: The intelligence of growth. *Theory into Practice, 23*(1), 26-34.

Keller, J. M. (1983). Motivational design of instruction. In C. M. Reigeluth (Ed.), *Instructional design theories and models: An overview of their current status*. Hillsdale, NJ: Lawrence Erlbaum.

Knox, A. B. (1986). *Helping adults learn*. San Francisco: Jossey-Bass.

McLagan, P. A., & Suhadolnik, D. (1989). *Models for Human Resource Development Practice (the Research Report)*. Alexandria, VA: American Society of Training and Development.

Minoli, D. (1990). *Telecommunications technology handbook*. Norwood, MA: Artech House.

Minoli, D. (1993). *Enterprise networking: Fractional T1 to SONET, Frame Relay to BISDN*. Norwood, MA: Artech House.

Moore, M. G. (Ed.). (1990). *Contemporary issues in American distance education*. Elmsford, NY: Pergamon.

Moore, M. G. (1993). Is teaching like flying? A total systems view of distance education. *American Journal of Distance Education, 7*(1), 1-10.

Neil, S. (1998, June 8). "Lights, camera, action!" Videoconferencing has become the star at a handful of companies. *PC Magazine*, pp. 69-72.

Newton, H. (1991). *Newton's telecom dictionary*. New York: Telecom Library.

Ontario Society for Training and Development. (1976). *Canadian training methods*. Toronto: Author.

Ontario Society for Training and Development. (1982). *Competency analysis for trainers: A personal planning guide*. Toronto: Author.

Paprock, K. (1993). *Learning for survival: A system approach to learning, change, and adaptation*. Unpublished doctoral dissertation, Education Division, Texas A&M University, College Station.

Paprock, K. E., & Williams, M. (1993). Instructional design in distance education. *Education Journal, 7*(4), j17-j19.

Paul, L. (1998, June). News and trends: Virtual conferencing. *Healthcare Informatics*, p. 16.

Popper, K. R. (1972). *Objective knowledge*. Oxford, UK: Oxford University Press.

Portway, P., & Lane, C. (1992). *Technical guide to teleconferencing and distance learning*. San Ramon, CA: Applied Business Telecommunications.

Rogers, C. (1961). *On becoming a person*. Boston: Houghton Mifflin.

Rowntree, D. (1990). *Teaching through self-instruction: How to develop open learning materials* (Rev. ed.). New York: Nichols.

Rupinski, T. E., & Stoloff, P. H. (1990). *An evaluation of navy video teletraining (VTT)*. Report presented to the Center for Naval Analyses, a Division of Hudson Institute. Alexandria, VA.

Spragins, J. D., Hammond, J. L., & Pawlikowski, K. (1991). *Telecommunications protocols and design*. Reading, MA: Addison-Wesley.

Tele-Systems Associates. (1994). *Distance learning network technology and applications update*. Report to the Rural Electrification Agency (REA), May 16.

Thach, C. E. (1994). *Perceptions of distance education experts regarding the roles, outputs, and competencies needed in the field of distance education*. Unpublished doctoral dissertation. Texas A&M University, College Station.

Thelen, H. (1960). *Education and the human quest*. New York: Harper & Row.

Toffler, A. (1971). *Future shock*. New York: Bantam.

U.S. Army. (1974). *U.S. Army TRADEP*. Washington, DC: Bureau of Training.

Van Doren, G. (Ed.). (1977). *Mortimer J. Adler: Reforming Education: The opening of the American mind*. New York: Macmillan.

Wang, M. (1990). *Metropolitan microwave network design and implementation*. Englewood Cliffs, NJ: Prentice Hall.

West, C. K., Farmer, J. A., & Wolff, P. M. (1991). *Instructional design: Implications from cognitive science*. Englewood Cliffs, NJ: Prentice Hall.

Williams, M. (1994). *Faculty development in distance education for continuing medical education: A baseline study*. Doctoral dissertation, Texas A&M University, College Station.

Williams, M., Smith, G., & Myers, D. (1995, Second Quarter). Texas A&M University Health Science Center/NASA Distance Learning Project. *Texas Journal of Rural Health*, pp. 14, 49-57.

Wolcott, L. L., & Burnham, B. H. (1991, August). *Tapping into motivation: What adult learners find motivating about distance instruction*. Paper presented at Seventh Annual Conference on Distance Teaching and Learning, Madison, WI.

Index

ARCS (Attention, Relevance, Confidence, and Satisfaction Model), 11-12, 108, 124, 125
Asynchronous learning environment, 4
Asynchronous transfer mode (ATM), 48-49
Attention, Relevance, Confidence, and Satisfaction Model (ARCS), 11-12, 108, 124, 125
Audiographics, 61, 66-68

Barriers:
    implementation of distance learning and, 20
    technology transfer and, 76-79
Broadband integrated services digital network (BISDN), 48
Bulletin board systems (BBS), 4, 8, 62-64, 68-70
Bus topology, 40

Case studies:
    audiographics (telematics), 61-72

    faculty development, 54-60
    technology transfer process, 81-87
CATV (cable TV systems), 44
Coaxial cable, 44
Communication, visual. *See* Visual communication
Community development, 17, 20
Competencies, core:
    conventional education, 24-26, 26 (table)
    distance learning, 27-29, 28-29 (table)
Computer graphics, digitized, 101-102
Computer-assisted instruction (CAI), 62, 71-72
Computer-based training (CBT), 4
Computer-mediated conferencing (CMC), 4
Concepts in distance learning:
    barriers to implementation, 20
    cost structure, 22-24
    distance vs. conventional, 15-16, 21, 111, 130-131, 144-145
    education delivery systems, 14
    future education systems, 17-18

informal education/community
  development, 17, 20
information technologies, 20-21
national policies, 19
regional overview, 18-19
teacher training, 16-17, 19
trends and issues, 14-15
Cost structure, 22-24

Distance learning, 2, 3
  ARCS model and, 11-12, 108, 124, 125
  asynchronous learning environment, 4
  audiographics (telematics), 61-72
  competencies, 27-29, 28-29 (table)
  levels of activity in, 3-5, 4 (figure)
  multimodel design, 8-9, 33, 54-56
  network growth, 6-7, 7 (table), 14-15
  roles and team membership, 30-32, 31 (table)
  synchronous learning environment, 4
  teachers' attitudes towards, 10
  technology in, 3-6
  telecommunication technologies, 50-51, 52-53 (table)
  See also Competencies, core; Concepts in distance learning; Education; Instruction design; Network setup

Education:
  core competencies, 24-26
  informal, 17, 20
  roles in education and training, critical, 26-27
Electronic mail (E-mail), 62

Faculty development, 54-60
Fiber optics, 44-45
Funding mechanisms, 22-23

Governmental policies, 19

High-speed data networking, 49-50

Information technologies, 20-21
Infrared links, 46-47
Instruction design, 105, 106
  distance learning and, 112, 123-124
  engaging students, 127-131
  image, personal, 121-122
  learning modes, 109-111, 110 (table)
  learning, meaningful, 106-107, 109 (figure), 133
  messaging style, 116-120
  participation, extent of, 107-108, 109, 110 (table)
  teacher preparation, 113-116
  teaching methods, participative, 124-127
  teaching models, 107, 109 (figure)
Integrated-services digital network (ISDN), 42-44
Interconnection architecture/protocols, 36
  OSI (Open systems interconnection), 36-38, 37 (table)
  SNA (Systems network architecture), 39
  SNMP (Simple network management protocol), 39, 50
  TCP/IP (Transmission control protocol/Internet program), 38
International Council for Correspondence Education (ICCE), 2
Internet, 5, 8
  TCP/IP (Transmission control protocol/Internet program), 38
  videoconferencing, 50

Just in time/just enough team approach, 54-60

Layout. *See* Visual communication
Learning:
  distance vs. conventional, 15-16, 21, 111, 130-131, 144-145
  engaging students, 127-131
  meaningful, 106-107
  messaging style and, 116-117
  modes of, 109-111, 110 (table)
Local area networks (LANs), 3, 38

Media. *See* Transmission media

Messaging style, 116-120
Microsoft, 5
Microwave links/short-haul radio, 45-46
Moore, Michael, 30-31
Multimodel design:
   distance learning, 8-9, 33
   support team members, 54-54-56
   teaching materials/media in, 97-103, 103 (table)

Network growth, 6-7, 7 (table), 14-15
Network setup:
   design questions, 65, 73
   high-speed data networking, 49-50
   interconnection architecture/protocols, 36-39, 37 (table)
   telecommunication technologies, 50-51, 52-53 (table)
   topologies, 39-41
   transmission media, 41-49

Open learning, 2, 3
Open systems interconnection (OSI), 36-38, 37 (table)
Open universities, 2, 18
Overhead projection, 100

Participation, 3-5, 4 (figure), 107-108, 109, 110 (table), 127-131
Popper, Karl R., 76
Protocols. *See* Interconnection architecture/protocols

Radio, short-haul, 45-46
Research:
   ARCS model, 11-12, 108, 124, 125
   competencies and roles, 24, 27
   learners and distant learning, 10-11
   teachers and distance learning, 10
Ring topology, 40-41
Rogers, Carl, 77, 80
Roles in training and development:
   conventional education, 26-27, 27 (table)
   distance learning, 30-32, 31 (table)

Simple network management protocol (SNMP), 39, 50
Slides, 35 mm, 100
Star topology, 41
Synchronous learning environment, 4
Systems network architecture (SNA), 39

Teacher training, 16-17, 19, 33, 113-116
Teaching:
   distance learning and, 10
   faculty development, 54-60
   materials/media in multimodel design, 97-103, 103 (table)
   professionals in multimodel project, 85-87
   teleteaching basics, 93-96, 93 (table)
   See also Instruction design
Technology transfer process, 76
   comfort/discomfort balance, 79-80
   fear, reactions to, 78-79
   perceptions as barrier, 76-78
   resistance to change, overcoming, 81-87
   teleteaching, 93-96, 93 (table)
   workspace, instructor/learner adapting, 87-91, 90 (figure)
Technology, 3, 18-19, 23
   future of, 5-6
   information, electronic, 20-21
   levels of, 3-5, 4 (figure)
   multimodel learning design, 7-9
   networking capabilities, 6-7, 7 (table), 14-15
   student population and, 23-24
   teacher use of, 23
   telecommunication, 50-51, 52-53 (table)
   See also Network setup; Technology transfer process
Telecommunication technologies, 50-51, 52-53 (table)
Telematics. *See* Audiographics
Telephone transmission, 41-42
Teleteaching:
   audio and video, 93
   equipment testing, 95
   peripheral audio checklist, 96
   support services reference guide, 94
   teaching tools, 98-103, 103 (table)

164 DISTANCE LEARNING

See also Communication, visual; Instruction design; Teaching
Topologies, network, 39
  bus topology, 40
  ring topology, 40-41
  star topology, 41
Transition, institutional:
  faculty development, 54-60
  See also Network setup; Technology transfer process
Transmission control protocol/Internet program (TCP/IP), 38
Transmission media, 6, 41
  ATM (Asynchronous transfer mode), 48-49
  BISDN (Broadband integrated services digital network), 48
  coaxial cable, 44
  fiber optics, 44-45
  infrared links, 46-47
  ISDN (Integrated-services digital network), 42-44
  microwave links/short-haul radio, 45-46
  telephone lines, 41-42
  VSAT links (Very small aperture terminal), 47-48
  See also Network setup
Transparencies, 100
Twisted pair (copper), 41-42

Verbal information into visual communication, 135-145
Very small aperture terminal (VSAT), 47-48
Videocassette recorder (VCR), 98
Virtual classrooms, 4, 5
Visual communication, 136, 144
  color selection, 141-142
  font selection, 139-141
  line options, 143
  space, parameters of, 137-139

Web. *See* World Wide Web
Wide area networks (WANs), 3
World Wide Web (WWW), 3, 5

About the Authors

Marcia L. Williams is currently Director of Telemedicine at the New York Eye and Ear Infirmary in New York City. She earned her undergraduate BS degree from Duquesne University and her MEd degree in corporate Training and Development from Pennsylvania State University. She received her PhD in Educational Human Resource Development from Texas A&M University. Her area of specialization is faculty and curriculum development for distance learning environments. During the past 15 years, she has accumulated a wide range of experiences with faculty and curriculum development in the diverse fields of education, health care, business, and government. Past work experiences include distance learning and telehealth consultant for an international manufacturer of interactive mediaconferencing equipment, as well as teaching in both universities and health care institutions. Her background includes training and consulting in Australia, Canada, Europe, Malaysia, Singapore, and Mexico.

Kenneth Paprock is on the faculty at Texas A&M University and works with Mexico and numerous Latin American countries as the International Coordinator for Educational Human Resource Development. He received the 1995 University Award from Texas A&M University for his contribution to supporting international programs. He also coordinates the Training and Development academic specialty and directs the Training and Development Certification Program at Texas A&M University. He earned his undergraduate and master's degrees from UCLA and holds a PhD in Adult, Higher and Continuing Education from the University of Illinois. He has 20 years' experience in human resource development in business, industry, and health care. He has consulted, lectured, and taught across the United States and internationally in Mexico, Hong Kong, Germany, Greece, England, and Scotland. His works have been published in the United States, Mexico, France, England, Canada, Yugoslavia, and Rumania.

Barbara Covington is currently a faculty member with Webster University, Ft. Leonardwood, Missouri, and a health care systems software/database trouble shooter for Mellott and Associates in Houston, Texas. She earned her undergraduate BS degree from the University of Florida, her Masters degree from the University of Pennsylvania, and her PhD in Educational Human Resource Development from Texas A&M University. She has more than 26 years of experience in civilian amd military health care, distance education, and health care informatics training, development, and program design. She is a retired U.S. Army Colonel. She has traveled and taught extensively throughout the world, most recently in Germany, Panama, and Mexico.